Henry's Wives

(The much-married musical)

Book, music and lyrics by
Leslie Bricusse

Samuel French — London
www.samuelfrench-london.co.uk

Copyright © 2006 by Stage and Screen Music B.V.
All Rights Reserved

HENRY'S WIVES is fully protected under the copyright laws of the British Commonwealth, including Canada, the United States of America, and all other countries of the Copyright Union. All rights, including professional and amateur stage productions, recitation, lecturing, public reading, motion picture, radio broadcasting, television and the rights of translation into foreign languages are strictly reserved.

ISBN 978-0-573-08129-3

www.samuelfrench.co.uk
www.samuelfrench.com

For Amateur Production Enquiries

United Kingdom and World excluding North America

plays@samuelfrench.co.uk

020 7255 4302/01

Each title is subject to availability from Samuel French, depending upon country of performance.

CAUTION: Professional and amateur producers are hereby warned that HENRY'S WIVES is subject to a licensing fee. Publication of this play does not imply availability for performance. Both amateurs and professionals considering a production are strongly advised to apply to the appropriate agent before starting rehearsals, advertising, or booking a theatre. A licensing fee must be paid whether the title is presented for charity or gain and whether or not admission is charged.

The professional repertory rights to this play are held by Samuel French Ltd, 24-32 Stephenson Way, London NW1 2HD.

The professional rights to this play are controlled by Stage and Screen Music B.V.

No one shall make any changes in this title for the purpose of production. No part of this book may be reproduced, stored in a retrieval system, or transmitted in any form, by any means, now known or yet to be invented, including mechanical, electronic, photocopying, recording, videotaping, or otherwise, without the prior written permission of the publisher. No one shall upload this title, or part of this title, to any social media websites.

The right of Leslie Bricusse to be identified as author of this work has been asserted by him in accordance with Section 77 of the Copyright, Designs and Patents Act 1988.

CHARACTERS

Henry
Catherine Parr
Anne Boleyn
Catherine Howard
Catherine of Aragon
Anne of Cleves
Jane Seymour
Thomas Wyatt - *doubles with*:
  Smeaton
  Thomas Culpepper
Wolsey
Norfolk
Will Somers
Thomas Cromwell
Elizabeth

Plus **Courtiers, Young People, Ladies-in-Waiting, Monks**, etc.

The action of the play takes place on an open stage and is set during the years of Henry VIII's reign up to the ascension of Elizabeth I.

MUSICAL NUMBERS

ACT I

No. 1	**The Perfect Woman**	Henry
No. 2	**Husbands and Wives**	Henry, The Six Queens
No. 3	**Without a Woman**	Henry
No. 4	**To Love One Man**	Catherine of Aragon
No. 5	**Get Rid of Her**	Henry
No. 6	**I'm Not!**	Anne Boleyn
No. 7	**The Grape and the Vine**	Henry, Smeaton
No. 8	**A Woman is a Wonderful Thing**	Henry
No. 9	**In Bed!**	Will Somers, Norfolk, Wolsey, Company
No. 10	**My Son**	Henry
No. 11	**The Grape and the Vine (Reprise)**	Smeaton, Anne Boleyn, Henry, Jane
No. 12	**Get Rid of Her (Reprise)**	Henry
No. 13	**Young Together**	Catherine of Aragon, Anne Boleyn, Jane Seymour
No. 14	**I'm Not! (Reprise)**	Catherine of Aragon, Anne Boleyn, Jane Seymour
	The Grape and the Vine (Reprise)	Henry

ACT II

No. 15	**Kings and Clowns**	Will Somers, Henry
No. 16	**Could Anything Be More Beautiful?**	Henry
No. 16a	**Could Anything Be More Beautiful? (Reprise)**	The Six Queens
No. 17	**Bitch!**	The Six Queens
No. 18	**The Very, Very Best of Friends**	Henry, Norfolk, Cromwell
No. 19	**The Perfect Woman (Reprise)**	Henry, Queens, Norfolk, Cromwell, Company
No. 20	**Henry Tudor**	Will Somers, Company
No. 21	**Is Sad**	Anne of Cleves
No. 22	**Get Rid of Her (Reprise)**	Henry
No. 23	**Ten Wishes**	Catherine Howard, Young People
No. 24	**The Wishing Tree**	Catherine Howard

No. 25	**Henry Tudor (Reprise)**	Will Somers, Company
No. 26	**The End of Love**	The Six Queens
No. 27	**A Man is About to be Born**	Henry
No. 28	**Sextet/Young Together (reprise)**	The Six Queens

No. 29 Finale
    The Grape and the Vine (Reprise)   Catherine Parr
    Henry Tudor (Reprise)   Will Somers, Company
    My Son! (Reprise)   Henry
    I'm Not! (Reprise)   Elizabeth

Vocal Score and Orchestral Parts for this musical are available on hire from Samuel French Ltd

Applications to perform this play by Professional Repertory (Stock) companies and by amateur performers in the USA and Canada should be made to Samuel French Inc, 45 West 25th Street, New York, NY 10010. USA.

First Class Professional Rights are controlled by Grakal and Bond, 1541 Ocean Avenue , Suite 200, Santa Monica, CA 90401, USA

PROLOGUE

The entire back wall is dominated by the famous Holbein portrait of Henry the Eighth

As the CURTAIN *rises, a younger, more virile Henry is* DC, *feet apart, hands on hips, glaring arrogantly at the audience, seemingly searching for someone. He is simply dressed in billowing white shirt and breeches*

A vibrant musical pulse starts under and builds. Henry sings. As he does so, the six Queens appear, dimly visible in a row behind him, evenly spaced across the stage, in order of succession (i.e. Catherine of Aragon first, and Catherine Parr sixth). All are dressed entirely in white, like a row of ghosts. As the lyrics of the song make more specific references to them, they become more clearly focused and react accordingly, both individually and collectively

Song 1: The Perfect Woman

Henry The perfect wife
For the perfect man
Is a difficult thing to see.
A woman who'd build
The perfect life
For a difficult king like me!

A lady of countless qualities,
Too intricate to explain;
The beauty of an Anne Boleyn,
The wisdom of a Catherine,
The gentleness of Jane,
(*Wistfully*) My Jane!

(*Arrogantly again*) She'll need to be a princess!
An angel!
A whore!
And more!
Where is she? The perfect woman!
And tell me, why can't I find her?

Am I blinder than other men?
Do they know more than I?
Must all my life go by?
Wondering who? Wondering why?
Trying to see—in my mind's eye.
I see her so clearly,
Yes, really, in my mind's eye.

He becomes hesitant

She'll be blonde, or brunette
With blue eyes, and yet,
I wouldn't really mind if they were brown!
She'll be slender and tall,
Unless of course she's small!
And she'll wear her hair up, or down!
I see her so clearly,
Well, nearly, in my mind's eye!
No, I don't see her at all!

He tries to reassure himself

And yet I love her, the perfect woman!
I'd love her to be beside me,
And to hide me from loneliness,
And save me from despair.
But where is she?
Where?
The perfect woman…
Isn't there.

The song ends

Henry, frustrated, exits

ACT I

The music of The Perfect Woman *continues gently under as the six Queens advance* DS *in line abreast. As they do so, six sumptuous costumes of regal splendour descend from the ceiling, and the six ladies step into them. During the ensuing dialogue, they subtly secure the velcro backs of one another's royal garments. The Queens remain on stage throughout the play, commentating or watching as required. One of them—middle-aged, motherly, grey-haired—fusses over the others like a nanny. This is Catherine Parr, the first to speak, just as she'll be the last to go*

Catherine Parr (*primly*) Here we all are, then. That's it!
Anne Boleyn He's not here yet.
Catherine Parr (*soothingly*) He's probably busy.
Catherine Howard He always keeps us waiting.
Anne Boleyn That's part of it!
Catherine Howard Part of what?
Anne Boleyn The game! There was a time—I could play it much better than him.

Catherine Parr hands Catherine Howard a head-dress. She puts it on. Catherine Parr holds up a mirror for her to look at herself in

Catherine Howard Will I have to wear *that*?
Catherine Parr He'll expect it.
Catherine Howard What the hell for?
Catherine Parr You want to please him, my dear, don't you?
Catherine Howard Not particularly.
Catherine of Aragon (*looking around anxiously*) Are you sure he isn't here yet?
Catherine Howard I think we'd have noticed.
Catherine of Aragon I must talk to him. The moment he arrives, we must talk!

Anne of Cleves, a beautiful, funny girl, looks confused. She speaks with a German accent

Anne of Cleves Is this the right place?

Anne Boleyn The right place for what?
Anne of Cleves I don't know what he means by it ... bringing me all this way.
Catherine Parr You'll get used to it, dear.
Catherine of Aragon *We* all had to!
Jane Seymour (*nervously*) Where's my darling? Have you seen my darling?
Anne Boleyn Your darling's not here yet.
Jane Seymour Where *is* he?
Anne Boleyn I thought probably with you.
Catherine of Aragon He may be with someone—none of us has even thought of.
Catherine Parr He may be alone.
Aragon/Boleyn/Cleves/Howard (*simultaneously*) Henry? Ha!
Jane Seymour He said he couldn't live without me.
Anne Boleyn He said he'd die if I kept him waiting a minute longer.
Catherine Howard He said he'd grow old without me.
Catherine Parr He *wanted* to grow old *with* me.
Anne Boleyn He did!
Catherine of Aragon Without me, he said, he felt a fool.
Anne Boleyn With you, he behaved like one!

The Lights fade. A distant fanfare of trumpets. The Queens are almost in darkness. The fanfare grows louder, more majestic

A golden shaft of Light, C. In it a man is standing, once again with feet apart and hands on hips. But this time in a glorious golden costume. White feather in his hat. Jewelled codpiece—the man triumphantly "stage-managed" as Henry the Eighth

The Queens see Henry and respond accordingly

Catherine of Aragon My husband!
Anne Boleyn My lover!
Jane Seymour My king!
Anne of Cleves My friend!
Catherine Howard My clown!
Catherine Parr My child!
Henry My God!

The Queens all start talking at once as Henry saunters forward

(*To the audience*) Of course, they complain. They grumble all the time. But have you noticed one thing about them? They're here! Every night. On time. Ready and willing, for marriage! Look at them! Eagerly climbing

Act I

into their costumes. Try and keep them away? It's impossible! Of course they've got no idea what they're taking on. Not like me... (*He takes off his hat with a flourish*) Not like King Henry. Oh, I may dazzle them with an ostrich feather and a diamond-studded codpiece ... but, as you can see, I take marriage extremely seriously.

Catherine Howard and Anne Boleyn are giggling together

Not like them! For me, marriage is a labour compared to which ruling a country is but a game of tennis on a Sunday afternoon...

The wives are all giggling as they finish dressing

...A battle we fight naked without armour. A cathedral which husbands must build with their bare hands.

The group of wives stop laughing, as Catherine of Aragon answers Henry

Catherine of Aragon *And* wives!
Henry Husbands!
Queens (*in unison*) *And* wives!

Song 2: Husbands and Wives

Henry Husbands and wives
Husbands and wives,
Sometimes I wonder how marriage survives!
But somehow it does.
And somehow it thrives
Thanks to wonderful husbands, it thrives!
Wives Thanks to wonderful, wonderful wives!
Catherine of Aragon Do you know why it is you never stay wed!
Catherine Howard And why you always seek a new bed?
Catherine Parr Cos while other men are seeking wisdom or bread
Anne Boleyn The King seeks nooky instead!

A collective gasp of shock from the other five wives

Jane Seymour Whatever Henry does, his feelings...
Catherine of Aragon Outbursts...
Anne Boleyn Hormones...
Jane Seymour ...Rule his head!
Anne of Cleves No wonder you never stay wed!

Wives	And always choose to seek a new bed!
Henry	Husbands and wives
	Husbands and wives,
	Choosing a partner's like juggling with knives!
	For each move we make,
	We're risking our lives!
	It's a marvel how marriage survives!
Wives	But it does!
Henry	Thanks to husbands!
Wives	And wives!

Catherine of Aragon Do you know why it is your image will fade?
Anne of Cleves You don't wage war—or lead a crusade!
Catherine Parr There are other kings who seek new treasures or trade!
Anne Boleyn But you just want to get laid!

Another gasp of shock at Anne's audacity

Jane Seymour Whatever Henry wants, he gets because he prayed!
Catherine Howard No wonder he always gets laid!
Anne Boleyn He's just too *tired* to lead a crusade!

Henry glares at the wives, shrugs and spreads his hands

Henry	Husbands and wives!
Wives	Husbands and wives!
Henry	Marriage is something the female contrives
	To master the male
	Like bees do in hives
	She conspires and cajoles and connives!
Wives	What a blessing for husbands!
Henry	And wives!
Wives	And husbands!
Henry	And wives!
Wives	And husbands!
Henry	And wives!

A handsome young man, Thomas Wyatt, enters as the song ends

Wyatt And friends, naturally!
Henry (*clasping Wyatt's hand, beaming*) And friends, indeed! Before I went into the marriage business, my life was filled to overflowing with wonderful, loyal, devoted, *true* friends... *Men*, naturally!

Three men enter the scene. Wolsey, an old fat man, dressed in scarlet, who

Act I

is the King's lawyer and cardinal. The young man who has just spoken, who will play the lovers of his wives (Smeaton, Culpepper, etc). And a hearty middle-aged uncle, who usually appears as the King's uncle Norfolk

Among the wives, Catherine of Aragon is being dressed in a white bridal veil

Wolsey Every marriage needs a friend.
Wyatt When you get bored staring into each other's eyes, you'll want to ask a friend to dinner. Someone unattached.
Wolsey Never be without a lawyer.
Norfolk There's nothing more useful than an uncle with a home in the country.
Wolsey Unless you've got a decent lawyer, she'll get her pretty fingers on every penny.
Norfolk Come down for the hunting. After a couple of weeks with a woman, it's such a relief to be able to *kill* something!
Wyatt I can give her those little attentions you no longer have time for, Henry.
Wolsey Wolsey, the friendly lawyer.
Norfolk Norfolk, the friendly uncle.
Wyatt Thomas Wyatt, the friendly friend.

The sound of a bell ringing us, *monks chanting. The three friends put a white jacket on Henry*

Wolsey Of course, I loved both of them!
Norfolk Catherine seemed a nice enough girl, for a foreigner.
Wyatt White bosom. Long legs. Cold though, for a Spaniard.
Wolsey I knew from the beginning the divorce would never be easy.
Norfolk Where the hell is Aragon? Somewhere up in Yorkshire, isn't it?
Wyatt That's Harrogate, Your Grace.
Norfolk Ah.

A huge crucifix is brought on by the monks

The Queens are all behind Catherine as bridal attendants. The friends are behind Henry, Wyatt as his best man. Henry is facing the audience, as is Catherine. As Henry speaks to the audience, the Queens mutter their comments

Henry I was not yet eighteen years old when I wed the widow of my brother Arthur. I was tall. Sprightly. I could outleap any man. And I was light-footed in the dance...

Catherine Howard I don't believe it.

Henry ...With a giant appetite for Surrey capon, Kentish oyster, pickled trout, Rhenish wine, and the joys of fornication.

Anne Boleyn Which hadn't yet brought him to carbuncles, gout, swollen leg...

Catherine Howard Or any grave disorder of the privates.

Henry I had only to snap my fingers and the world would drop its skirts and lie down obedient. The dues of a perfect king.

Anne Boleyn Before his marriage, the King is said to have been notably timid in the presence of ladies.

Henry looks searchingly at the various ladies around him and sighs deeply as the music starts under

Henry But every king must needs find a queen ... especially this one! No man is an island—and certainly no king!

Henry flirts with his various wives-to-be as he sings

Song 3: Without a Woman

> I am a king,
> But more than that,
> I am a man,
> And, as a man,
> I keep on wondering,
> Wondering
> Why women are the one and only thing
> That truly make me feel I am a king!
>
> Springtime and health,
> Wisdom and wealth,
> A man may have them all.
> I have them all,
> But without a woman
> To feud with and fight with,
> And then to spend the night with,
> A man has nothing at all.
>
> Sunshine and rain,
> Passion and pain,
> A man may know them all.
> I've known them all,

Act I

> But without a woman
> To talk to and scream to,
> And dedicate his dream to,
> A man knows nothing at all.

Catherine of Aragon In your case, most certainly true, Henry.

Henry
> Glory and fame,
> Love and acclaim,
> A man may seek them all.
> I seek them all,
> But without a woman
> To laugh with and cry with,
> To live with and to die with,
> A man seeks nothing,
> A man knows nothing,
> A man has nothing
> At all.
>
> There is something
> About a woman,
> I could never be
> Without a woman!

Catherine Howard Well, according to the history books, you never *were*!
Anne Boleyn And the history books don't know the half of it!
Henry A king by divine right is to wed the perfect woman and to present to his overjoyed people a son and an heir to the throne. (*He joins his friends and looks ruefully at Catherine of Aragon. To Wolsey*) Right, uncle. Time to get married.
Wolsey A dream fulfilled, my lord. England at last in bed with Spain.
Norfolk I can think of a lot of things I'd sooner be in bed with than Spain.
Wolsey Be of good cheer, my Lord.
Henry I am of good cheer, my Lord.
Wolsey I have seen much of Spain, and she has a beautiful coastline.
Henry So has the Isle of Wight, but I wouldn't want to spend the rest of my life there!

Catherine of Aragon and Henry move together to stand in front of the monks. All sing Jubilate

Wolsey (*singing*) Jubilate, Amen.
All (*singing*) Jubilate, Amen.
Wolsey I now pronounce you man and wife.

Norfolk (*to Wyatt*) Which is more than she can do. She can't pronounce anything. Can never understand a bloody word she says.
Anne Boleyn The Queen was some six years older than her husband, which gave one or other of them a distinct advantage.
Catherine Parr It was quite a ceremony.

The Lights change

The monks go

Henry and Catherine move DS *separately*

Henry The ceremony was the last quiet thing about it.
Catherine of Aragon Pomp! Show! Ostentation! Vain delights!
Henry (*looking to Heaven*) Another sermon!
Catherine of Aragon Games, gambles, profligate spending...
Henry The people love me for it!
Catherine of Aragon It's the duty of a King to be feared. You lack the courage to be hated.
Henry Which makes *your* father the bravest man on earth!
Catherine of Aragon He has a certain dignity. You put yourself in a ridiculous position.
Henry God's teeth! We're born and die and make love in a ridiculous position. What is dignity?
Catherine of Aragon A kingly quality ... that I must teach you, Harry.
Henry Thank you ... *Mother*!
Catherine of Aragon *Child*!
Henry Mind your tongue! I'm your King!
Catherine of Aragon And I your wife!
Henry My bonds! My constriction! My sour-faced confessor, whose joy is to see me gloomy.
Catherine of Aragon Whose hope is to see you wise.
Henry My rack!
Catherine of Aragon Your conscience!
Henry My penance!
Catherine of Aragon It's late, Henry! Come away to bed.
Henry To bed with you? I'd rather have myself scourged and say three decades of rosary!

Catherine of Aragon moves US

Henry and Catherine. At first they said we were like two lovebirds locked in the same golden cage. Twenty-four years that marriage lasted! Till we were more like two tigers, clawing at each other's throats!

Act I

Lighting change, and attitude change, to denote the passage of time

Anne Boleyn, with the Queen's nightgown over her arm, enters the royal bedchamber, ready to help her mistress undress

Catherine of Aragon (*weary of her nightly cry of twenty-four years*) Come to bed, to your wife, Harry. Else you may be tempted.
Henry (*looking at Anne Boleyn*) There's no sin in temptation. What say you?
Anne Boleyn (*curtsying, lowering her eyes*) I am not tutored, Sire ... on the subject of sin.
Henry Mistress...
Anne Boleyn No, Sire. No-one's.
Henry No, no. I mean your name.
Anne Boleyn Ah. Anne Boleyn, Sire.
Henry Anne Boleyn. Ah, yes. Mary's sister. Very nice.
Catherine of Aragon (*calling*) Harry!

Anne Boleyn hurries away

Henry smiles wickedly. The Lights fade to darkness. Catherine of Aragon is heard uttering a torrent of passionately angry and incomprehensible Spanish. The Lights come up. Henry stands beside Catherine of Aragon. She's reading a piece of paper ... a legal document. Henry is looking at her. He seems embarrassed

Henry I have told them you consent to the divorce.
Catherine of Aragon It's not true! *Madre di Dio!*
Henry (*exasperatedly*) Why would you cling to me—against my will?
Catherine of Aragon Because I'm part of you. Why does your right arm cling to you? Would you lop off your right arm?
Henry For the good of my kingdom, I would lop off anything I had to... (*Sotto voce*) Including your head!
Catherine of Aragon Who worked for you, brought you up?
Henry I no longer need a nursemaid, thank you.
Catherine of Aragon I helped you, Harry. Through your struggles and the blunders of your youth.
Henry So, is that any reason to stay and haunt my old age?
Catherine of Aragon I was there when you couldn't hold your pint of claret ... and vomited on the shoes of the Spanish Ambassador!
Henry (*roaring*) I want a woman who's never seen me vomit!
Catherine of Aragon I gave you everything I had!
Henry So you are spent. There's nothing left!
Catherine of Aragon Everything you wanted!

Henry (*roaring again*) I wanted a *son*! A man is entitled, surely, to his one small piece of immortality!
Catherine of Aragon I tried … I tried for you! The miscarriages … the deaths … the bleeding … my womb's been a battlefield … strewn with the corpses of your so-called love. (*She is crying*) You did love me once.
Henry (*understanding*) Love you? Of course I loved you! It will always be so with us… With both of us… Those years… remember Nonesuch? Our first summer… God, I have given you … such wonderful memories, Catherine. Golden moments.
Anne Boleyn For you to keep pressed between the pages of your Bible…
Catherine Howard While he presses the next young lady between his thighs…
Henry Women have no memories. They always think that what's over never happened. No one can take away those afternoons at Nonesuch, Catherine. I shan't forget them.
Catherine of Aragon I always wanted to make you happy.
Henry So … here's your opportunity. (*Shouting*) Consent to the divorce!

Henry storms out

Catherine, deeply hurt, retains her composure. Music under

Song 4: To Love One Man

Catherine of Aragon Easy to leave, hard to stay,
How many marriages end that way?
Easy to stay, hard to leave,
That is much more what I believe;
It's so hard to leave…

The sun deserts the day,
But he'll return.
The daylight drifts away,
And leaves the night to yearn.

The clouds can come and go,
The way they please.
For me it isn't so,
For me the rules are these.

To make each day
The best I can,
And in my life
To love one man,

Act I

> And hold him close and warm,
> Through good and ill,
> To ride life's little storm,
> And be together still.
>
> I want to end
> As I began,
> And in my life
> To love one man.
>
> Easy to leave, hard to stay,
> How many marriages end that way?
> Easy to stay, hard to leave,
> That is much more what I believe.
> It's so hard to leave.

Henry storms back in and stands glaring at Catherine

Henry Well?
Catherine of Aragon (*quietly*) My conscience would never allow me to consent to the divorce.
Henry My conscience is as tender as yours. I can't *sleep* for worry over the sin we are committing!
Catherine of Aragon (*incredulously*) *Sin*?!
Henry Lying together for our lust ... with no son to show for it! Man is not made for pleasure, merely.
Catherine of Aragon My church tells me it would be a sin to divorce you.
Henry My God tells me it would be a sin *not* to! For a king to die barren and unfulfilled—*that* is mortal sin, surely?!
Catherine of Aragon Find a church to tell you that!

Catherine leaves as Wolsey enters

Henry grabs Wolsey's arm. The other Queens are looking after Catherine, except for Anne Boleyn, who is looking at Henry

Henry Must I live and die under the dark cloud of her perpetual disapproval?
Wolsey What are your instructions, Sire?

Henry starts to pace up and down

Henry I must be seen to act with the wisdom and foresight befitting a King of England!

Song 5: Get Rid of Her

(Singing)   When a woman drives you
To the edges of insanity,
When each thought
You think of her's
A landmark of profanity,
When you even loathe
The brilliant portrait
Holbein did of her,
The moment has arrived
To get rid of her!
(Roaring at Wolsey) D'you *hear* me?
Get *rid* of her!

Wolsey *(bowing low)* Your Majesty.

Henry   Get rid of her,
Get rid of her,
Just send her back to Spain!
I never want to see
Her medi-evil face again!
Nor listen to her preaching
Like some sanctimonious squid!
This Aragon's
A paragon
Of whom I must be rid!

I'll be rid of her moans
And her grumbles and her groans
And her old spanish bones
In my bed! *(He smiles at Anne Boleyn)*
Then that wondrous young thing,
In the first flush of spring,
More befitting a king,
Can get in there instead!

(Back to Wolsey) Get rid of her,
Get rid of her,
That bible-thumping cow!
I want my cake and eat it,
And I want to eat it *now*!

Act I

> So stuff her with paella
> And then ship her to Madrid.
> Stick her in a barrel
> And then batten down the lid,
> And send her,
> With the compliments of England,
> To El Cid!
> Get rid of her,
> Get rid of her,
> Get rid,
> Get rid,
> Get rid!

At the end of the song Wolsey and Henry exit together, deep in legal consultation

Catherine of Aragon comes back DS, controlling her tears

Anne Boleyn comes to meet her. The other Queens are standing around them. The stage darkens

Catherine of Aragon Where's the King, Mistress Boleyn?
Anne Boleyn With the Cardinal, discussing business, my lady.
Catherine of Aragon Business? What business?
Anne Boleyn I know not, my lady.
Catherine Howard Nonsense. She knows perfectly well. (*She whispers to Jane Seymour*) It's the divorce!
Jane Seymour Divorce! Is that how it ends?
Catherine Howard If you're lucky.
Catherine of Aragon Are you in love, Anne? Have you a favourite?
Anne Boleyn Oh yes, Madam. I have a favourite.
Catherine of Aragon And you would wish to marry this man?
Anne Boleyn If it should please *him* to marry *me*, your Majesty—then, yes, with all my heart!
Catherine of Aragon How wise you are—to want to please him so!

Catherine of Aragon goes

Anne curtsies, then shrugs at the other Queens and Ladies-in-Waiting

Anne Boleyn And *tease* him even more!

The music starts under

During the song Henry enters

Song 6: I'm Not!

Anne Boleyn Is it a crime to tease the King?
Not if you know you please the King.
I'm well aware that he's the King.
And he's well aware of me!
Wouldn't you say?
Couldn't you tell?
Didn't you see? (*She fondles her breasts*)

When he caught sight of these, the King,
I saw a spasm seize the King!
He would have liked a squeeze, the King,
And I would have liked it, too!
Hell, wouldn't you?
Well, wouldn't you?
Nell, wouldn't you?

Women are hypocrites,
Pity of pities!
So lacking in wit,
They'd never admit
That men like pretty titties,
And long legs, and hips,
And love's delicious lips!

I made him ill-at-ease, the King.
But I will not appease the King!
I'll have him on his knees, the King,
Which might be a right good thing!

(*Aside, wickedly*) Then we'll *both* go down in history!

Women in general, even my sisters,
Think that I'm a whore!
Simply because I'm aware
And approve
Of what my body is for!

But no man shall touch me,
Save one of high degree!

Act I

God save the King
For *me*!

Women are afraid to be
Half the things they're made to be,
Why are they ashamed to be
All the things I've aimed to be?
I'm not! I'm not!

Why do they pretend to be
Paragons of modesty,
Figures of fidelity,
Models of morality?
I'm not! I'm not!

I know what men like!
What men like is *me*!
But they get frustrated
When they can't have what they see!

I know what I want!
What I want's the King!
But of course I want him
With a crown
And with a ring!

I do not pretend to be
Sweetness and simplicity,
Dreaming domesticity,
Duped by men's duplicity!
I'm not! I'm not!

My ideas on life,
Fill all my friends with dread,
But they'll thrill his majesty -
Especially in bed!

Let other ladies
Let their lives go by!
I'm not!
Not I!

Anne exits

Henry watches her go. He confides in the audience

Henry Anne, my lady unobtainable. Her skirts fell, but never the temple of her virginity. All fire above and ice below! Oh husbands, pray that you may be spared from the onslaught of a promiscuous virgin! (*He moves* US *and stands with his back to the audience*)
Catherine Howard Did he say virgin?
Jane Seymour Is that what he thought she was? *Ha*!
Catherine Parr On the subject of women—His Majesty was sometimes *far* from perceptive! (*From the clothes-rack she takes a scarlet dress, buttoned high up to the neck, in which she re-dresses Anne*)

The Queens are talking to Jane

Catherine of Aragon When I wanted to make love, he'd stay up for hours ... discussing the Protestant movement in Germany.
Anne of Cleves At night the King would kiss my hand and say "Goodnight, sweetheart"! And in the morning he would say "Good morning, dollink"! He never discovered that after sex I became beautiful!
Catherine Parr He thought I just wanted to sit by the fire reading the Bible ... I'd have liked the occasional game of cards!
Anne of Cleves I would have just liked the occasional!

Smeaton, a young musician, enters DS *playing a lute. He is playing very softly as though he were composing, experimenting and repeating phrases, playing the tune of* The Grape and the Vine

Catherine Howard Down the dale and up the tree,
        The King had me
        And the King had me!
        He slept alone occasionally.
Anne of Cleves In my country we have a saying: "If you're going to play with your schnitzel, there's no point my serving the strudel"!
Anne Boleyn (*looking at her askance*) You're not English, are you?
Jane Seymour I think Henry understands me perfectly...

Anne Boleyn, dressed in scarlet, turns to face the audience

Anne Boleyn He thought I was cold, white, and unobtainable as a snow-tipped mountain...
Catherine of Aragon He totally ignored my Spanish sensuality.
Anne Boleyn ...It was a belief I did nothing to discourage.

Henry turns to face the audience and moves DS. *Smeaton is now playing the tune more clearly*

Henry I have been studying how I may best thaw my ice-lady. Some subtle heat ... no fire of lust to frighten her.

Smeaton (*singing*) As the grape will cling to the vine...

Anne of Cleves What is that music?

Smeaton A little trifle I am composing.

Anne of Cleves It is beautiful. Play it for me.

Smeaton (*singing*) As the grape will cling to the vine
        As the vine will cling to the walls of the house
        As the house will cling to the earth
        And the earth to the sea
        I will cling to thee, my love...
        I will cling to thee.
        Together we make the sweetest wine...

Henry (*listening*) *Music!* I will compose a song for my lady unobtainable.

Smeaton (*singing*) Like the grape and the vine, my love...

Henry A song on the subject of constancy.

Smeaton (*singing*) Like the grape and the vine.

Henry Master Smeaton. Smeaton ... come here.

Smeaton Your Majesty?

Henry There is an air ... floating in my head. I know not whence it comes, but it is a pretty humming.

Smeaton Will your Majesty let me hear it?

Henry You may find the fingering for this, Smeaton.
  (*Singing*) As the grape will cling to the vine
        As the vine will cling to the walls of the house...

Smeaton (*protesting*) But, your Majesty...

Henry Be quiet. I'm composing, Smeaton.
        As the house will cling to the earth
        Tiddey-pom tiddey-pom
        I will cling to thee, my love
        Tiddey-pom tiddey-pom...
  A pretty start, is it not?

Smeaton (*with grim resignation*) I could not better it.

Henry Better it? Of course not! Your task is to note it down, Smeaton. As Master of my Music, yours is the drudgery, mine the inspiration ... now do be quiet.
  (*Singing*) Together we make the sweetest wine...

Smeaton Exquisite.

Henry A simple metaphor ... taken from horticulture. (*Worried*) No bawdy meaning can be spelled into it?

Smeaton None, my Lord.
Henry Pity.
   (*Singing*)   Like the … grape and the vine…
Smeaton (*singing*) …My love
         Like the grape and the vine…
Henry You like it, Smeaton?
Smeaton Very much, Sire.
Henry Then I am doubly glad I composed it! And I shall sing it after dinner!

Henry goes off, singing the song

All the Queens except Anne Boleyn form up behind Catherine of Aragon as her Ladies-in-Waiting and stand behind her on one side of the stage. Anne Boleyn in her scarlet dress is on the other

   Norfolk and various Courtiers and Ladies of the Court, dressed as for an evening party, come chattering in

   Smeaton is DS with his lute and has been joined by other musicians who are providing the music

The Grape and the Vine *starts playing softly and continues throughout this scene*

Catherine Parr I wonder at her impertinence…
Catherine Howard Flaunting it…
Anne of Cleves She has bewitched the King, Madam, surely…
Catherine Howard Notice her left hand … the shadow of a sixth finger!
Catherine Parr Buttoned almost to the chin…
Anne of Cleves Her neck's too long. It's her worst feature.
Catherine of Aragon She has good eyes.
Catherine Howard The eyes of a sorceress!

   Henry enters in a new splendid costume

Everyone bows. The music stops temporarily

Henry Tonight the King's guests will dance to the King's music! (*He waves a hand*)

The music starts again. Henry addresses the song blatantly to Anne Boleyn

Act I   21

Song 7: The Grape and the Vine

Henry A good king loved a lady fair,
With passion strong and true.
The lady was inclined to doubt.
And told him:
If you love me, sir,
Pray tell how much you do!
And the good King told her true.

As the grape will cling to the vine,
As the vine will cling to the walls of the house,
As the house will cling to the earth,
And the earth to the sea,
I will cling to thee,
My love,
I will cling to thee.

Together we make the sweetest wine,
Like the grape and the vine,
My love,
Like the grape and the vine.

Wolsey enters

Wolsey What is this caterwauling? It's terrible!
Norfolk The King wrote it.
Wolsey It's *beautiful*! Quite beautiful!
Catherine Parr Our King has all the talents.
Anne of Cleves Give him another quiet afternoon and he'll invent the bicycle.
Wolsey (*impressed*) This is *your* music, your Majesty?
Henry (*modestly*) An air that came to me this afternoon ... as I walked in the garden. A pleasant trifle...
Norfolk (*to Wolsey*) Well, at least it rhymes.
Wolsey Ssh, my Lord. Listen to the music.
Norfolk I'd sooner listen to the cry of a good pack of hounds.

Henry stares defiantly at Smeaton as he continues singing

Henry The lady was enchanted
By her regal troubadour.
Though still she was inclined to doubt.

She told him: "I have never heard
Such wondrous words before!"
So the good King told her more.

He gestures to Smeaton to continue the song while he talks to Anne Boleyn. Smeaton sings over the ensuing dialogue

Smeaton As the fruit will grow from the tree,
As the tree will grow
From the heart of the seed,
As the seed will grow from the fruit,
And the fruit from the tree,
I will grow from thee, my love
I will grow from thee.
Together our hearts will intertwine,
Like the grape and the vine,
My love,
Like the grape and the vine.

Henry The lady knew
The handsome King
Was quite the best of men!
No more was she inclined to doubt,
For he said:
"You will be my queen,
Although I'm not sure when!"
And the good King sang to her again.

Henry snaps his fingers for Smeaton to sing the refrain

Smeaton As the sun is true to the sky,
As the sky is true to the stars and the moon,
As the moon is true to the month,
And the month to the year,
I'll be true to thee, my dear.
I'll be true to thee.

Company I vow to be thine,
And thou be mine
Like the grape and the vine,
My love,
Like the grape and the vine.

Act I

Now the Chorus is singing, repeating the refrains quietly. There is a Lighting change and a dance starts—a stately Court galliard. Henry holds out his hand, starts dancing with Anne Boleyn. Catherine of Aragon, frozen-faced, stands on the other side of the stage, watching them

Henry The lady was unkind to doubt. For one year I have been struck by the dart of love. Am I your lover, your friend? Am I anything at all?
Anne Boleyn I'm sorry, my Lord ... if I have wounded you...
Henry You have the power to dress my wounds.
Anne Boleyn I cannot guess your Majesty's meaning.
Henry Bind them tightly ... in your bed sheets, Anne.
Anne Boleyn If I could.
Henry And with your mouth, heal up my scars...
Anne Boleyn If I were free.
Henry Free? You *are* free!
Anne Boleyn Not while *she*'s still Queen, your Majesty.
Henry She is my queen only in name ... I swear it!
Anne Boleyn The name is what I want from her.

The dancers change partners. Henry is dancing with Catherine of Aragon

Henry I've always had the greatest respect for you, Catherine.
Catherine of Aragon Respect. I can't sleep with your respect.
Henry You are wise ... beyond all women...
Catherine of Aragon Can my wisdom keep me warm at night? If I let you go, what will be left to me?
Henry You'll have your religion ... and all the new books. Perhaps you'll take up gardening.
Catherine of Aragon Why don't you tell *her* to take up gardening? I hear she has six green fingers!

Norfolk and Wolsey are talking together, watching the dancers. Norfolk is drinking

Norfolk Divorce going well, is it?
Wolsey The King's great matter is suffering certain delays at the hands of H.H.
Norfolk H.H.?
Wolsey His Holiness—the Pope.
Norfolk Oh yes, him. Little Italian fellow—handbag with the smoke coming out. It makes me sick to think of the King of England asking favours of a greasy little wop! It's against the scriptures!
Wolsey Are your religious views influenced at all, my Lord of Norfolk, by

the fact that Mistress Anne Boleyn is your niece? I should point out to you that should the lady share his Majesty's bed, it could be of inestimable value to all three of us!

Norfolk Wolsey—that suggestion is totally amoral, highly irreligious ... and very good thinking. I'll see what I can do.

Wolsey I was sure that a man of your incomparable intellect and integrity would grasp the point eventually, your grace.

Wolsey sweeps away

Norfolk (*grumbling to himself*) Bloody Cardinal! Always making jokes about religion. He's only *in* the Church for the money and those pretty red frocks!

Norfolk exits

Henry is dancing with Catherine of Aragon

Catherine of Aragon So you want me to disappear ... to vanish.

Henry I want you to be happy.

Catherine of Aragon Reading Greek and pruning roses in a nunnery. I'm sorry, Henry. I'm your wife! I can't just vanish in a puff of smoke. Even to please your Mistress Longneck!

The dancers change partners. Henry is dancing with Anne Boleyn

Henry The divorce goes speedily.

Anne Boleyn So you told me two years ago.

Henry My lawyers are striving tirelessly.

Anne Boleyn I suppose we may eventually lie together—under a slab of marble in Westminster Abbey! So passionate, my lord. To invite me to share your tomb!

Henry I ache for you, Mistress.

Anne Boleyn I ache also.

Henry My body burns.

Anne Boleyn I too have a fire inside me. Henry, the divorce...

Henry, mad with desire for her, is by now completely carried away

Henry Come away to bed, sweet Anne.

Anne Boleyn (*innocently*) To bed? I'm not tired.

Henry So I may make love to you. Till the stars fall out of your ears.

Anne Boleyn Is that what you want?

Act I

Henry Would you not pleasure your King?
Anne Boleyn Pleasure your Majesty? With all my heart!
Henry (*greatly relieved*) Praise be to Jesu!
Anne Boleyn The moment the divorce is final.
Henry (*furiously*) Anne, I *command* you!

The music and dancing ends suddenly. The Lights change

Anne Boleyn Oh no, my lord! Go and command your lawyers!

Anne smiles sweetly, curtsies, and is gone, leaving Henry in a towering rage

Angry music starts under

Henry (*roaring*) God's blood, that bitch negotiates more fiercely than the King of France! (*Yelling after Anne*) Perhaps you should marry *him*! (*During the following he paces up and down in fury and frustration*)

Song 8: A Woman is a Wonderful Thing

(*Singing*) What can you say
About a woman who is vicious
And malicious and ambitious,
Avaricious and suspicious?
I mean, what can you say?
What can you say?

When a woman's superstitious,
Injudicious and officious,
Surreptitious and capricious,
And in every way delicious!
I mean, what can you say?
What can you say about a woman like that?

His anger suddenly subsides in a wave of romanticism

Except that she is wonderful,
And beautiful,
As you can see,
Everything a woman should be!

A woman is beauty and humour and grace,

A daydream, a fable that falls on its face.
A glimmer of summer, a sparkle of spring,
A woman is a wonderful thing!

She's warmer than sunshine,
She's sweeter than youth,
As fickle as fortune,
As fragile as truth,
As rare as the rainbow tomorrow may bring:
A woman is a wonderful thing!

A man pretends the world is his.
She lets him think it is.
She knows that men are only boys.
She knows that children need their toys.

A man can be lonely,
Believe me, I know
And when he is lonely,
Where else can he go?
She smiles as she places him under her wing;
A woman is a wonderful thing!
A wise and warm and wonderful thing.

Furious, Henry strides away into the shadows

The Light isolates Jane Seymour, who walks to Anne Boleyn. They are together in a pool of light

Jane Seymour Not to pleasure his Majesty till you were safely wed? That was your policy?
Anne Boleyn (*bitterly*) My good, wise, cool, sensible policy!
Jane Seymour It succeeded?
Anne Boleyn Oh, yes. It succeeded. It got me *this*! (*She pulls open her dress—and for the first time we see, round her white throat, a thin scarlet ribbon, bright and clean as the cut of the axe*)

Darkness as Jane gives a small scream of fear

Jane Seymour Is that what happens?
Anne Boleyn If we don't go quietly.
Jane Seymour I've always said that a woman who lives with the man of her dreams must learn to live with the dreams of her man.

Act I   27

Anne Boleyn (*astonished at her naïvete*) You said that like you really believe it!
Anne of Cleves In my country we have a saying—"If you don't like pickled cabbage, stay away from the sauerkraut factory"!

Henry is at the end of his tether with Catherine of Aragon

Henry No more talk, Catherine. We are *divorced*!
Catherine of Aragon (*accusingly*) You found no church to sanction that!
Henry (*triumphantly*) I not only *found* one, I *founded* one! Behold, The Church of England!

Molto pomposo church organ music

Wolsey enters, dressed as the Archbishop of Canterbury, followed by Norfolk in a surplice

Catherine of Aragon Why is Cardinal Wolsey dressed up in that ridiculous costume!
Henry That is *not* Cardinal Wolsey! That is the Archbishop of Canterbury, Head of *my* Church of England!
Catherine of Aragon (*contemptuously*) The Church of England! Huh! Article I. "Thou *shalt* commit adultery!"

Catherine of Aragon sweeps out

Henry, in his nightgown, goes US *and gets into bed with Anne Boleyn*

Henry (*gleefully*) So much for Catherine of Arrogant!
Catherine Howard Why couldn't he just *sleep* with Anne, without getting so *religious* about it?
Anne of Cleves (*sighing*) Men take these things too seriously. It was heroic, really.
Catherine Howard He gritted his teeth, and became a martyr to his faith.

Norfolk and Wolsey move DS *together—as Henry and Anne Boleyn start to make love under the sheets and the musicians play* Onward Christian Soldiers

Norfolk (*with relish*) The Church of England, eh? What a jolly clever wheeze!
Wolsey Thus are new religions born, my lord. I think I'm growing too old

for all these games. To create the Church of England headed by his Majesty, we have to have a rift with Rome.
Norfolk A punch-up with the Pontiff, eh? Splendid!
Wolsey (*stiffly*) It's called a Reformation, my lord.
Norfolk As long as there's a bit of a war, I don't care *what* you call it!
Wolsey Reformation is a religious term meaning to do what the King tells you! Watch and you will see!
Henry (*shouting from the bed*) Thank you, Lord, for the Church of England! In which a just God will at last most surely give the King a *son!*
Catherine Howard He's on about a son again!
Anne of Cleves This extraordinary ambition to reproduce himself.
Anne Boleyn As though one of him weren't enough!
Anne of Cleves Out of each of us he wants there to pop a miniature Henry!
Catherine Howard Complete with a feathered hat and a tiny be-jewelled codpiece!
Catherine Parr Marvellous at hunting and irresistible to women!

The King's jester, Will Somers, enters strumming his lute. He observes Henry and Anne Boleyn cavorting in the bed

Norfolk Ah! The King's Fool—the wisest man among us! What say you to all this, Will Somers?
Will Somers (*considering*) Question, my lord. What is the most important thing in your life? Your mother? Your father? Your children? Or your wife? (*He shakes his head*) Answer? *None* of them!

Song 9: In Bed!

(*Singing*)   Three score years and ten, they say,
              Is man's allotted span,
              And one score years and more of them
              He spends where he began!
              It's fated from the moment of your birth;
              A bed's the most important place on earth!
              How many tender memories
              It offers us to keep,
              The least of which is sleep!

As the song progresses, Will Somers is joined first by Norfolk and Wolsey, and eventually by the entire Company

              Where does your mother conceive you?
              In bed!

Act I   29

>   Where does your wife deceive you?
>   In bed!
>   Where do most things happen
>   That can alter all our lives?
>   And where do men spend half their time
>   When they're not with their wives?
>
>   Where does a maiden see trouble ahead?
>   In bed! Of course!
>   But what would she rather be doing instead?
>   No matter which way you view it,
>   Though you know you may live to rue it,
>   It's nice if she's there to stay and do it
>   In bed! In bed! In bed!

Will/Norfolk/Wolsey Where are decisions of state made?
>   In bed!
>   Where are the best laid plans laid?
>   In bed!
>   Where do future kings and things
>   First see the light of day?
>   And nine times out of ten,
>   Where do old soldiers fade away?
>
>   Where does a dreamer start dreaming?
>   In bed!
>   Where does a virgin start screaming
>   In dread?
>   Opinion may be divided
>   But since Adam and Eve collided,
>   The fate of the world has been decided
>   In bed! In bed! In bed!

Will/Various Company Where is a coward a hero
>   Or so I've read,
>   In bed!
>   Where was great Nero a zero?
>   'Tis said!
>   Where's the place most married couples
>   Choose to recommend?
>   The same place their divorce starts
>   When he screws his wife's best friend!

Where is the battle of life waged?
From A to Zed,
In bed!
But where would you sooner have staged it
Instead?

I know of no great arena
Where the scenery is serener!
The miss not to miss
Is misdemeanour in bed!
In bed! In bed! In bed!

Company If man's gonna kill his brother,
And if Father won't talk to Mother,
The least we can do is love each other
In bed! In bed! In bed!

It's not such a mystery,
History happens in bed!

Anne Boleyn gives a little delighted cry

Anne Boleyn It's happened! I am with child!
Will Somers (*to the audience*) What did I tell you?

Will Somers exits

Henry How long?
Anne Boleyn Five minutes.
Henry I feel it... Yes. A son! (*He climbs out of bed*) I know it! It is a son!

Anne gets out of bed. She is hugely pregnant

Wolsey (*making a hasty blessing*) I now pronounce you man and wife.

Anne goes back to the Queens. Henry goes to his gentlemen, who put a crown on his head

Catherine Howard It was a very quiet ceremony.
Catherine of Aragon It had to be!

Catherine Parr goes out and returns with a loose velvet gown

Act I

Henry walks towards Anne. Wolsey is holding a huge and heavy crown US

Anne Boleyn If it's a girl, I want to call her Elizabeth.
Henry (*firmly*) It will *not* be a girl. Nothing is too good for the mother of my son. We must show the world, Anne … my son's mother is my true Queen…

He leads her to the bishop, who slowly places the enormous crown on her head

   My country's Queen… Queen of my heart!

Anne is swaying, hardly able to bear the weight of the crown

Anne Boleyn Do you want him to be *exactly* like you?
Henry Exactly like me, but without my mistakes!
Catherine of Aragon (*incredulously*) Mistakes! *You* made *mistakes*?
Henry (*to Anne*) I didn't marry you soon enough. Catherine was a mistake … old enough to be my mother.
Catherine of Aragon (*furiously*) I'd have had to be *six*!
Henry I'll get him some ponies sent out of Wales. We can ride after the red deer together. And my man Farris will make him a suit of armour.

Anne gasps and gives a cry of pain

Anne Boleyn Does it really *have* to be a son?
Henry Oh yes! It really *does*! Henry the *Ninth*!

Henry stands and sings proudly and cheerfully as Anne Boleyn, with the Queens and a Doctor round her, goes through the agonies of childbirth

Song 10: My Son

   At last,
   The son I've dreamed of,
   Hoped for, prayed for,
   For many a year.

   At last, thank God,
   This prince, this King,
   My son
   Will soon be here!

And on that day
My world will be secure,
And England will endure.

My son, my son,
My son will be a prince,
Of that you may be sure.
Attractive and intelligent,
Perceptive and mature.

My son, my son,
Too handsome to be true,
As witty as can be,
Compassionate and lovable
And kind to a degree
Is he,
My son.

A lover of the arts,
A spirit bold and free,
A hold on women's hearts
That is incredible to see
Has he,
My son.

Beloved of the gods,
Determined and defiant,
Possessed of every gift and grace.
A king, a giant.

My son, my son.
And everyone who meets him
Will readily agree
That my son is exactly like me!
That's why he is my son!

The Doctor takes a small bundle from the bed and hands it to Henry

Catherine Parr Your daughter, my lord.

Henry opens the clothes and looks into the bundle

Act I 33

Anne Boleyn Elizabeth… (*To Henry*) Well, don't blame *me*! It's not *my* fault! I thought you *liked* girls!
Henry (*in a terrible voice*) Don't mock me, Anne!

Catherine Howard takes the baby firmly from Henry. The Queens all crowd round, admiring the baby, cooing over it, and totally ignoring Henry. Excluded, he walks DS, as the Queens go on fussing over the baby, ad libbing "Who is beautiful? Just like her mother. Who's going to be Queen of England, then?" etc. as they push the bed off the stage

Anne Boleyn (*cynically*) His Majesty the Devoted Father promptly left for Wolf Hall in Wiltshire to indulge himself in his most favoured pastime—The Chase!

Catherine Parr takes Jane Seymour by the hand and leads her to a distant US corner, where she takes off Jane's head-dress, and fits a pair of antlers to her head. Henry is being dressed by the Courtiers for hunting, and given a hunting spear

Henry I was looking forward to a keen day's hunting—or an hour in the tilt-yard with my old friend, Thomas Wyatt—being, at that time, in fine physical condition.
Catherine of Aragon Less so since the divorce.
Henry And a king greatly loved by the highest and most lowly in his realm.
Catherine of Aragon Less so since the divorce.
Henry I was thirty-three years old.
Catherine of Aragon You were forty-two and *looked* it after the divorce.
Anne Boleyn His second marriage was undergoing certain … tensions.
Catherine of Aragon After the divorce it all seemed to become a little *desperate*!

Henry kneels and prays

Henry Dear God, please grant me a son. Grant me a wife—a true and loving wife, a woman of beauty, intelligence, truth, charm and humour—of good breeding stock, decent family, stinking rich and preferably a Sagittarian.
Wolsey *And* a virgin!
Henry A virgin? In England?
Norfolk We've found one for you, Sire.
Wolsey Intact?
Norfolk No, in Kent.
Wolsey She's called Jane Seymour.

Henry is quickly on his feet. The courtiers start a low, murmuring clapping

Courtiers Rut! Rut! Rut! Rut! Rut!

The shouting of "Rut!" gets louder, like a ritualistic Gregorian chant. The Courtiers form two lines and are beating on the ground with their spears and bows, making as much noise as possible. From the US corner Catherine Parr releases Jane Seymour, who runs like a hunted deer between the beating, shouting rows of Courtiers. She runs through them and then is hidden. All we can see are her antlers behind the Courtiers. Henry moves so he is looking down the line—hunting for Jane. The confusion of the hunt ensues

One of the ladies of the court strips off Jane's clothes except for a leotard and, still wearing her antlers, red ribbons of blood at her throat, tied by her wrists and ankles to a pole, she is finally carried before Henry by two Courtiers, followed by the others in triumphant procession. Catherine Parr removes the antlers and replaces Jane's dress

Henry's spear is tipped with red, as if he's just killed the deer. Jane Seymour, now without her antlers and demure in her Tudor dress, comes towards him, hesitant

Henry You don't care for this sport, Mistress Seymour.
Jane Seymour I find it fearful ... and yet with a strange excitement...
Catherine of Aragon Oh, he'll like that!
Catherine Howard He'll like it *very* much!
Anne Boleyn At his approach, we were *all* meant to be filled with a strange excitement!
Anne of Cleves *Meant* to be!
Henry And your king. How do you find your king?
Jane When I come before him and he has his spear in his hand—I am again fearful.
Catherine Howard This girl is either *incredibly* stupid, or brilliant beyond belief—I'm not sure which!
Henry No need of that, my chuck. His spear may be bloody... (*He hands his spear to Wyatt*)

Wyatt takes the spear, bows and goes

But his ways are gentle.
Anne Boleyn (*incredulously*) Did he say *gentle*?
Catherine Howard Gentle when he starts ... until he feels his way up to your neck.

Act I

Henry This bright March morning ... this finger-freezing, sun-dazzling, skirt-lifting, windy morning ... with the late frost snapping the twigs in the woods of Wolf Hall... I feel on a sudden born again.
Catherine of Aragon Oh, not again!
Henry Would you trust me, Jane? Would you trust me with your happiness?
Anne Boleyn His record is not exactly encouraging.
Catherine Howard I mean, would you put an habitual embezzler in charge of the Bank?
Jane Seymour (*to Henry*) I might think sometimes, my lord, of your ladies past.
Henry Past ladies I regard as so many prison sentences ... which mercifully were not for life!
Anne Boleyn (*outraged*) A prison sentence! *Me*?
Catherine of Aragon With him, there's certainly no time off for good behaviour!
Henry (*to Jane*) But even the *worst* criminal, Jane, is allowed another chance when he has served his sentence ... and God knows, I've served mine! None of us, to be sure, is judged beyond redemption.
Catherine Howard If she falls for *that*, she'll fall for anything!
Henry I would ask you to overlook my tragic past experiences ... as I make all allowance for your virginity.
Catherine Howard Is she a virgin?
Catherine of Aragon That is a matter of some controversy.

Henry kisses Jane's hand. Then he rises to his feet

Anne Boleyn Rubbish! No child can pass through the hot tumble of the Seymour nurseries and carry her virginity like an unbroken egg to her first communion. Impossible!
Henry Those past ladies, Jane ... you should have heard the complaints. Not enough money! Not enough attention! Not enough love! I don't know why they should have complained...
Anne Boleyn Shall we tell her?
Catherine Parr In a minute.
Henry But the moment it was finished, it was as though I had driven them out of Paradise.
Catherine Parr There he goes again...
Catherine Howard Confusing himself with God.
Henry Mere marriage was never exciting enough for them. They had to have their plots ... or their politics ... or their little adventures up the back stairs to the waiting gentlemen.
Anne Boleyn (*to Catherine of Aragon*) Were you ever able to keep a lady-in-waiting who wasn't actually *deformed*?

Catherine of Aragon Quasimodo's sisters were my permanent staff!
Henry Whereas I...
Anne Boleyn Whereas he...
Henry Would have been quite contented with the peaceful estate of monogamy... that single choice, so clear and perfect... so that when a man and woman grow old... When they hug their knees to the fire, for they are too spent for hunting... And suck the bone, for they are blunt-toothed and cannot chew the flesh... Then they may remember some such March morning in Wiltshire... Which was their beginnings.
Jane Seymour (*besotted*) Oh, Henry!
All the Queens (*in unison, mimicking her*) Oh, Henry!
Anne Boleyn That's exactly what he said to me!
Catherine of Aragon And me! And he said it to me *first*!
Catherine Howard (*her mind made up*) She is incredibly stupid! I *thought* so!

Smeaton enters, playing The Grape and the Vine *on his lute, and singing it to Anne Boleyn*

Song 11: The Grape and the Vine (Reprise)

Smeaton   As the grape will cling to the vine,
As the vine will cling to the walls of the house,
As the house will cling to the earth,
And the earth to the sea,
I will cling to thee, my love,
I will cling to thee.
Anne Boleyn That's the king's song.
Smeaton No. It was of *my* composing, Lady. Your husband stole it away from me.
Anne Boleyn He used *your* song ... to seduce *me*! He was wooing me ... secondhand! It would seem that he needs help in *everything*!
Smeaton I felt I was singing it to you, my lady ... even if it was his voice.
Anne Boleyn Your voice speaks more clearly of love.
Henry (*to Jane*) I have composed a song—for my lady unobtainable.
Jane Seymour (*delightedly*) For *me*? You have written a song for me?
Henry There is an air floating in my head. I know not whence it comes, but it is a pretty humming...
   (*Singing*)   As the sun is true to the sky,
      As the sky is true
      To the stars and the moon,

Smeaton (*singing to Anne*) As the moon is true to the month,
   And the month to the year,

Act I 37

> I'll be true to thee, my dear,
> I'll be true to thee.

Henry (*singing to Jane*) I'll be true to thee.

They finish the song as a quartet

Henry/Jane/Smeaton/Anne I vow to be thine,
> And thou be mine.
> Like the grape and the vine,
> My love,
> Like the grape and the vine.

Smeaton Where's my Lord?
Anne Boleyn Out hunting.
Smeaton Far away?
Anne Boleyn Far, *far* away! (*She puts out her hand, touches him*) You are so thin, Smeaton. (*She looks round, excited, delighted by their danger*) Careful. Is someone there?
Smeaton It was nothing.
Henry (*to Jane*) I must have your answer, Jane. Jane, I must have it!
Smeaton I have looked in many places … and only in my Lady Anne have I found perfection.
Anne Boleyn For this afternoon.
Smeaton Who cares about tomorrow?

Henry and Smeaton sing to their ladies together the last verses of The Grape and the Vine. *At the end, Smeaton kisses Anne, Henry kisses Jane. While Smeaton and Anne continue to kiss, Henry and Jane move* US *together*

As Smeaton is kissing Anne, Norfolk enters, and stands looking at them

I love … my Lady Anne. (*He looks round, sees Norfolk, gives him a look of terror*)

The stage darkens rapidly, sound of a scream, the scream increasing, as Smeaton is tortured in the dark

Norfolk Repeat. I have stolen the King's wife.
Smeaton I have stolen…
Norfolk And have committed fornication…
Smeaton And would have committed fornication…
Norfolk And *have* committed…
Smeaton And have committed … *fornication*!

Lights up. Henry, furious, is pacing in front of Anne Boleyn, Norfolk in attendance, the Queens in the background

Henry Smeaton! A little musician...
Anne Boleyn He could do what you couldn't!
Henry What?
Anne Boleyn Make up a song of his own!
Henry And others ... have there been others?
Anne Boleyn Do you imagine, my lord, that only men go hunting?
Henry Who? Tell me *who*?
Anne Boleyn Young men. All *young* men! Thin, with small buttocks and soft shy voices. They say you were timid once.
Henry *Names*! Tell me their names!
Anne Boleyn Norris and Weston in my bed. Oh, and Brereton under the stairs. Thomas...
Henry Thomas?
Anne Boleyn Thomas Wyatt. Times without number ... in the tilt-yard ... when you had both done jousting.
Henry *Thomas*? My *friend*?
Anne Boleyn You played at tilt with merry Thomas. So did I!
Henry Whore! Traitor! Lying, treacherous whore! Would you spit on your marriage vows? Is there no faith left? No true love *anywhere*?
Anne Boleyn So I have my little Smeaton ... and you your little Seymour.
Henry (*a cri de coeur*) It's not the same!

Norfolk, obsequious, moves to Henry

Norfolk What is your pleasure, my lord, in the matter of the Queen?
Henry (*pondering*) The world looks to the King of England as the embodiment of justice and fair play!

Song 12: Get Rid of Her! (Reprise)

>Get rid of her!
>Get rid of her!
>Licentious little whore!
>The morals of an alley-cat
>And lovers by the score!
>
>The corpses of her paramours
>Will build a pyramid!
>And she shall shed

Act I

>That pretty head,
>Of which I will be rid!

>I'll be rid of her wiles,
>Her precocious little smiles,
>Which bewitched and beguiled
>And betrayed!

He smiles at Jane Seymour

>And I'll try, if I can,
>To bear grief like a man!
>Give my life to the plan,
>I'm dying to get laid!

He sees Norfolk's sudden frown

Henry No, no, Uncle Norfolk—I'm dying for the *plan* to get laid!
Norfolk (*realizing*) Ah!
Henry Get rid of her!
Get rid of her!
The evil, scheming slut!

(*To Anne*) That mouth forever open
Soon will be forever shut! (*He takes Jane's hand*)
And I can then reveal the love
That hitherto I've hid!

As the Guards lead Anne away

(*To Norfolk*) There goes
As good a pair of thighs
As ever I've bestrid!
There's scarce a bed in England
Into which they haven't slid!
Get rid of her!
Get rid of her!
Get rid!
Get rid!
Get rid!

Henry and Norfolk exit together, leaving Catherine of Aragon and Jane Seymour alone on stage with the other Queens in the background

Song 13: Young Together

Catherine of Aragon We were young together,
    We were springtime.
    We began together
    And we ran together
    Through the golden days
    Of youth.

Anne Boleyn enters to join them

Anne Boleyn And in truth, together
    We were happy.
    For we dreamed together
    And it seemed, together,
    We would see the years go by.
    But the golden days have flown,
    And we wander on alone.
    We were young together,
    You and I.

Jane Seymour We are young together,
    We are springtime.
    We will run together
    In the sun together,
    Through the golden days
    Of youth.

    For in truth, together,
    We are happy.
    We will grow together,
    And I know, together,
    We will see the years go by.
    And some sweet and distant day
    I will smile at you and say:
    We were young together,
    You and I.

Catherine of Aragon/Anne Boleyn But the golden days go by,
    And alone is how you die.
All Three   We were young together,
    You and I.

Act I

Anne Boleyn is prepared by the King's Guard for her execution. Jane Seymour is prepared by her Ladies-in-Waiting for her wedding

Jane Seymour moves slowly towards Henry

Wolsey as Archbishop of Canterbury enters and stands behind Henry

Henry puts out his hand to Jane and they stand in front of Wolsey, who marries them

Anne Boleyn, as she moves to her execution, sings the reprise of I'm Not! *as Henry sings* The Grape and the Vine

Song 14: I'm Not!
(Reprise)

Anne Boleyn Women are afraid to
    be
Half the things
They're made to be!
Why are they ashamed to be
All the things I've aimed to
    be?
I'm not!
I'm not!

I cannot pretend to be
Sweetness
And simplicity,
Dreaming domesticity,
Duped by men's duplicity!
I'm not!
I'm not!

Let other ladies
Let their lives go by
I'm not!
Not I!

The Grape and the Vine
(Reprise)

Henry As the grape will cling to the
    vine,
As the vine will cling
To the walls of the house,
As the house will cling to the
    earth,
And the earth to the sea,
I will cling to thee, my love,
I will cling to thee.

As the sun is true to the sky,
As the sky is true
To the stars and the moon,
As the moon is true to the
    month,
And the month to the year,
I'll be true to thee, my dear,
I'll be true to thee.
I'll be true to thee.

I vow to be thine,
And thou be mine,
Like the grape and the vine,
My love.

Anne Boleyn goes to the scaffold and her death and Henry to his third wedding and the arms of Jane Seymour. The CURTAIN and the axe fall together

ACT II

At the rise of the CURTAIN, *the positions are as at the end of Act I. The Lighting distinguishes the brilliant wedding group, Henry and Jane standing in front of Wolsey, who is marrying them, and Anne Boleyn, who is still kneeling with her head on the block. She's now wearing a black dress, with the thin red ribbon at her neck, and the executioner is relaxing, leaning on his axe as though his work were done. Henry is putting a ring on Jane's finger. She looks up at him, beautiful, excited, smiling radiantly. Everyone is congratulating them. Tableau*

Will Somers, the King's jester, enters and surveys this unlikely scene, strumming his lute

He regards the turbulent tableau before him with some amusement, bows deeply and deferentially to the audience, then sings to us as he meanders through the static stage picture

Song 15: Kings and Clowns

Will Somers Kings and clowns, kings and clowns,
The magic world of kings and clowns.
Like yours, it's full of ups and downs.
Fate smiles and frowns
On kings and clowns.

Clowns and kings, clowns and kings
Our lives are roundabouts and swings,
The storms and stings that fortune brings,
She also brings
To clowns and kings.

Gentlemen or jester,
It's just another name!
King or clown, boil it down,
All men are the same

Act II   43

> They love to play a game.
> It's all a game.
>
> One wears rags, one wears crowns,
> And one man swims and one man drowns.
> But fate won't worry which is which,
> For fate there is no poor or rich,
> The two can switch,
> And fools wear crowns!
>
> Such are life's ups and downs,
> Sunday smiles and Monday frowns,
> And brings you kings
> And clowns!

The music continues under. Will Somers stops beside Henry and Jane Seymour, looks at them closely, appraising them as a couple, then shakes his head dubiously

Will Somers I don't think this one's going to last, either! (*He pulls Henry away from Jane, bringing him to life*)

They continue the song together

          Kings and clowns,
          Clowns and kings!
Henry   Our kingdoms both are circus rings!
          While fools and villains pull the strings,
          The minstrel sings
          Of clowns and kings!
Will Somers Clowns are kings, kings are clowns,
          When romance does the regal rounds.
Henry   A simple wench makes simp'ring sounds,
          And blue blood pounds,
Will Somers And kings are clowns!
Henry   Pastry-maid or princess,
          It's just another name!
Will Somers Tart or queen, cool or keen,
          S'always been the same!
Will/Henry Girls love to play a game!
          It's all a game!
          Kings and clowns, clowns and kings,
Henry   Our lives are comic, fragile things!

                    But one thing we can say for sure,
                    The ladies, though not always pure,
                    Provide allure, which kings endure!
Will Somers Flashing eyes, plunging gowns,
Henry Winning wars on eiderdowns!
Will/Henry Ensuring kings are clowns!

Will Somers exits

The tableau breaks, and the wedding celebrations continue to the merry music of Kings and Clowns

Anne Boleyn slowly lifts her head from the block. She's smiling, a small secret smile as she looks at Jane. She stands up, smoothing the skirts of her black dress

Henry takes his new bride into his arms

Henry I didn't marry you soon enough, Jane.
Jane Seymour Oh, Henry!
The Wives (*in whispered mocking chorus*) Oh, Henry!
Henry Catherine was a mistake, old enough to be my mother! Anne was a mistake, young enough to be my daughter! But you, my darling sweetheart love, mother of my wonderful son-to-be, are totally and completely *perfect*! Now what do you say to *that*?!
Jane Seymour (*overwhelmed, stammering*) I—I—It's—it's perfect!
The Wives (*echoing her*) It's perfect!

Catherine of Aragon, also dressed in black, enters and joins Anne Boleyn

Catherine of Aragon (*acidly*) I think we may safely assume he didn't marry her for her wit!

As the music starts under...

Henry (*to Jane*) You have so many unique qualities these other women never had!
Anne Boleyn Especially boredom!

Song 16: Could Anything Be More Beautiful?

Henry   This land I love,
               This England,
               I love her like a woman,
               A sweet and gentle woman,

Whom I shall always treasure
And adore.

And now that I love you,
England is you,
And you are England, too!
No man could ask for more,
And I say to you
What I've said to her
So many times before.

Could anything be more beautiful
Than you are, than this is?
Could any time be more wonderful
Than now?

Could anything else replace
Your tender and warm embrace?
I look at your lovely face
And know somehow

That nothing will ever be to me
What you are this moment.
This moment will fill my heart
My whole life through.

Could anything ever be
As dear to me
As we two are?
Could anything be more perfect?
No, nothing's more perfect.
Could anything be more beautiful
Than you are?
You are
You are.

Henry is surrounded and congratulated by all the men. Jane is alone for a moment. She looks very happy. And then the two dead Queens, Catherine of Aragon and Anne Boleyn, come up to Jane and kiss her

Catherine of Aragon Congratulations! I know you'll be tremendously happy.

Jane looks at her, puzzled and alarmed

Anne Boleyn What's the matter, dear? Weren't you expecting us?
Catherine of Aragon We wouldn't have missed this for anything!
Anne Boleyn Wonderful to see two such radiant people.
Jane Seymour Thank you! Really! I'm so happy! Thank you.
Anne Boleyn You really *should* thank us!
Catherine of Aragon You do owe it *all* to us!
Anne Boleyn If he hadn't had such a hellish time with us, he'd never have been so delighted to settle down with you!
Jane Seymour I only hope I can make him happy.
Catherine of Aragon Oh, you won't find *that* difficult!
Anne Boleyn Not hard at all. I mean, you're a novelty! We'll keep an eye on you, dear. Just don't give him too many parties.
Catherine of Aragon Or too many clever answers.
Anne Boleyn He can't stand late nights.
Catherine of Aragon He detests arguments.
Anne Boleyn Just remember our mistakes. You'll be all right, my dear.
Catherine of Aragon We'll always be there, looking after you.

The crowd moves away. The other Queens are far us. *Jane and Henry are in their domestic bliss at Hampton Court. Anne Boleyn and Catherine of Aragon watch with increasing amusement*

Henry (*looking around*) So, Jane, how do you like Hampton Court?
Jane It's perfect!
Henry It was my old Uncle Cardinal's house. One of the most beautiful houses in England. That's why I took it off him. He certainly knew how to make himself comfortable! Lawns barbered to perfection, sweeping to the river. Sweet herb gardens ... glass-houses for white grapes and muscats. I must spend more time in the garden.
Anne Boleyn (*yawning*) What a thrill for you!
Catherine of Aragon The Empire's crumbling. The Pope's lost the voice of authority. All over Europe man is questioning his conscience ... and Henry's in the garden, pruning roses.
Anne Boleyn Given up girls ... and taken to pollinating melons!
Catherine of Aragon Waging a ruthless war against the greenfly in the rhubarb.
Anne Boleyn Melons don't answer back!
Catherine of Aragon The well-tended hyacinth is not promiscuous!
Jane Seymour (*enthusiastically, to Henry*) Gardening ... that would be perfect!
Henry Perfect!
Jane Seymour Sitting here in the evenings ... so peaceful.
Henry (*stifling a small yawn*) No-one coming to dinner.

Act II

Anne Boleyn He'll miss the banquets.
Henry With Anne every night was celebrated like Christmas!
Anne Boleyn Poor Henry! He found it so exhausting. (*To Jane*) He's much happier with a simple chop by the fire.
Jane Seymour I thought you'd like—a simple dinner.
Henry In Anne's day a hundred sat each night at table, with a band of music-players in the Great Hall—and then dancing ... till the sun rose like a pale ghost in the East window ... and the garden was full of empty goblets and young maids scuttling between the hedges.
Anne Boleyn (*smiling at him*) What a bore *that* sounds!
Jane Seymour She must have cost you dearly.
Henry *Dearly!*
Jane Seymour I think it's perfect. Just the two of us together. You do like chops, don't you?
Henry (*automatically gallant*) A mutton chop with you, Jane, is enough of a banquet. What need of Norfolk turkey stuffed with Surrey capon?
Anne Boleyn (*with relish*) With side dishes of pheasant, veal, woodcock, and guinea fowl.
Henry (*nostalgically*) Game pies and strawberries. Pig's head sharpened in a sweet sauce with a toothful of oranges.
Anne Boleyn Roast boar and marmalade. Young spitted lamb with apricots. Sparkling purple wines out of France.
Henry Golden Rieslings out of Germany. Rich dark Madeira and the blood-red wine from Portugal. Who needs all that?
Jane Seymour Would you like a cup of cocoa?
Henry (*blankly*) Cocoa?
Anne Boleyn Well, at least they've got each other!
Jane Seymour We've got each other.
Anne Boleyn And a mutton chop.
Henry Yes.

Long pause. Neither of them speaks

Jane Seymour I may not be able to arrange banquets like Anne did.
Catherine of Aragon Don't worry, dear! He thinks you're perfect.
Jane Seymour Have you—er—written any new songs lately?
Henry New songs, Catherine? Er—Anne? I mean *Jane*? I—er, have no need of new songs.
Catherine of Aragon He's got no-one new to sing them to! At the moment.
Henry My songs fought my battles for me. Now the war is over. I have won you, Jane.
Jane Seymour (*sighing happily*) Perfect peace.
Henry Yes. Perfect. (*He stifles another yawn*)

They both stare into space

    I was thinking…
Jane Seymour What?
Henry If it were Catherine … we should be arguing the business all night.
Jane Seymour What business?
Henry England's business.
Jane Seymour I hate arguments.
Henry Oh, so do I! (*Without conviction*) Really.
Jane Seymour I would never argue with you, Henry.
Catherine of Aragon What *will* you do in the evenings?
Henry (*throwing the opinion down like a challenge*) Thomas Cromwell is vain, sinful, devious and corrupt. He would make an excellent Chief Justice.
Jane Seymour I expect you're right, dear.
Henry You don't agree with me, do you?
Jane Seymour Of course, darling. Of course, I agree.
Henry It takes a corrupt Justice to really understand a thief!
Jane Seymour You're so wise, Henry! And you know so much about the law.
Catherine of Aragon So much he can invent a new one whenever it suits him!
Henry So much I can invent a new one whenever it suits me!
Catherine of Aragon That was *my* line, darling.
Jane Seymour I'd never *argue* with you, Henry.
Henry (*disappointed*) Never?
Jane Seymour Oh, no. *Never.*
Henry Crabbed Catherine would have disputed with me till daylight.
Anne Boleyn And Anne the Sorceress would have kept you up dancing.
Jane Seymour (*yawning*) Till daylight? I do need my eight hours sleep.
Catherine of Aragon (*yawning also*) Not exactly stimulating, is she, little Miss Perfection?

The quintet of Queens sing together in perfect harmony and with limitless vitriol. During the following, Henry dozes off

Song 16a: Could Anything Be More Beautiful? (Reprise)

The 5 Queens Could anything be more truly dull
              Than you are, Miss Seymour?
              Could any day be more dismal
              Than today?

Act II

>Could anything else replace
>Your singular lack of grace?
>I look at your dreary face
>In dire dismay!
>
>For no-one could be D-E-A-D
>As you are, this moment.
>This moment will dull my brain
>My whole life through!
>
>Could anything ever be
>As tedious as these two are?
>Could anything be more boring?
>No, nothing's more boring!
>Could anything be more truly dull
>Than you are?
>Yes, *you* are!
>Yes, *you* are!

Henry awakens with a start

Henry (*yawning profoundly*) Shall we go to bed?
Jane Seymour Only if you say so, my darling. (*She goes to him, puts her arm around him*) The stars are so clear. It'll be another sunny day tomorrow.
Henry (*desperately*) *Another*? No! Tomorrow I must—er—go on a journey, Jane ... to hunt with my Uncle Norfolk!
Jane Seymour (*hurt and puzzled*) Why?
Henry (*letting out all his frustration*) Because this weather's foul. We'll kill an evil-eyed, sharp-toothed old boar in the rain—and there's nothing whatever to do in the evenings but get drunk and quarrel ... and listen to my squalid political friends plotting to arrest each other for treason! Because... Oh, because no-one thinks it's *perfect*!

He slams away from the stunned Jane and strides US *to where a table with candlesticks and wine is being set*

Norfolk and Cromwell are sitting half drunk and in dirty hunting clothes at the table

Henry is given a cup of wine and drinks greedily. Sound of men laughing US. *Jane is alone* DS *and in tears in a golden patch of light*

Catherine Howard, looking very young and wearing a long white night gown, comes running out of the shadows and hands Jane a gardening basket, and then turns to speak quickly to the audience

Catherine Howard His Majesty stayed in the draughty castle of his Uncle Norfolk while the Queen stood alone in the garden, snipping dead heads from the roses.

She goes to run off, but Henry, who has noticed her immediately and is instantly enchanted by her youthful beauty, grabs her hand as she goes by

Henry God's mercy! And where do you think you're going?
Catherine Howard To bed. It's past my bedtime.
Henry (*admiring her*) I'm sure it is. Your name?
Catherine Howard Catherine.
Henry Catherine. Do you like arguments? Catherine what?
Catherine Howard Howard, and I like almost anything.
Henry (*puzzled*) Howard?
Catherine Howard Uncle Norfolk is my uncle, I *think* ... and your Queen Anne was my cousin! Why does that make you laugh?
Henry (*chuckling*) No matter. What games are you playing?
Catherine Howard Nursery rhyme games ... for children.
 (*Singing*)   Here comes a candle to light you to bed
         And here comes King Henry to chop off your head!

Catherine Howard runs away into the dark

Henry watches her go

Henry (*musing*) Another Catherine... Another Norfolk ... God save me!
(*He returns his attention to the Norfolk dinner table*)

Cromwell and Norfolk are quietly drunk—and a little complacent

Cromwell The state of the world has reached perfection! By the wisdom of His Majesty in counsel, we are free from the tyranny of the Pope ... and the threats of the Emperor!
Norfolk We have castrated the Cardinals...
Cromwell Skimmed the cream from the monasteries...
Norfolk People are contented, even in the Midlands!
Cromwell I've never known it so quiet...
Norfolk (*grumbling*) We need a jolly good war, if you ask me..

A sudden noise, teenagers laughing and giggling. An area DS *becomes the*

Act II

nurseries in Norfolk Castle. *It's full of very handsome teenagers in night gowns, boys and girls, who are dragging in small beds, pillow fighting and playing more amorous and less innocent bedroom games. Catherine Howard in her long white night gown, a ravishing black Lolita, is the obvious leader*

Henry (*laughing at Norfolk*) A war? You seem to have a war of your own, Uncle, going on upstairs.
Cromwell The nurseries!
Norfolk (*grumbling*) Young people!
Henry The Howard breeding ground. Sounds like you have a full kennel. You always seem to have an inexhaustible supply of beautiful young bitches in heat, Uncle Norfolk.
Norfolk My nieces, you mean?
Henry How many this season?
Norfolk (*vaguely*) At the last count? Oh, it slips my memory. Half a dozen, maybe.
Henry Why not brand them? A coronet on the rump for legitimacy.
Norfolk For a noble family to survive as long as mine has, Your Majesty, it must excel in *both* the war zones—the bedroom and the battlefield!

They roar with drunken laughter as the focus of light switches back to the five Queens—this time Catherine Howard is absent and Jane Seymour wears a black dress

Anne Boleyn If Henry so much as *sees* my young cousin Catherine Howard at Uncle Norfolk's castle, I fear once more for the future of his realm.
Catherine Parr That *child*? That innocent child?
Anne Boleyn That bitch! That world-class bitch!
Jane Seymour But she's barely *seventeen*! And *so* beautiful!
Anne Boleyn Exactly! She has *all* the qualities—and *none* of the inhibitions!
Catherine of Aragon Then God help England if he gets close to *her*!

Song 17: Bitch!

Anne Boleyn Beauty,
Catherine of Aragon Intelligence,
Jane Seymour Truth,
Catherine Parr Charm,
Anne of Cleves Humour,
Anne Boleyn These are the qualities in which she's rich!
 Put them together and spread the rumour:
 She's a B-I-T-C-H bitch!

> She would never spoil her sweet young mind by using it!
> She invested in her maidenhood by losing it!
> And she rose above her squalid life by choosing it!
> She's a lamb! She's a sham! She's a bitch!

Catherine of Aragon She will prove the pow'r of promises by breaking them.
> She will air her views on liberties by taking them.
> She'll acknowledge men of wealth and fame by making them.
> She's a dear, so sincere, she's a bitch!

The other Queens get the idea and join in with relish

Various Wives Nice young ladies
> Nurture a Nirvana wish,
> *This* young lady
> Nurtures a piranha fish!

Anne Boleyn She will calculate each move while she is viewing you.
> She is planning your destruction while coo-cooing you.
> She will radiate great charm while she is screwing you.
> She's a whore! What is more,
> As we pointed out before,
> First and foremost:

All 5 Queens She's a bitch!

The music continues under

Jane Seymour You don't *really* believe she's a bitch, that little mouse?
Anne Boleyn *Every* woman is a bitch! Some of us just never get a chance to *prove* it, that's all!
Anne of Cleves In my country we have a saying—"A woman is a bitch when other bitches believe all the bitchy things that other bitches say about her"!

The music builds

> She would never risk a precious friend by being one.
> She would never break a contract by agreeing one.
> She would never crave a crown, except by seeing one,
> She's a tease, a disease, she's a bitch!

Jane Seymour She'll respect your private letters by unsealing them.
> She will share your little secrets by revealing them.
Anne Boleyn She will learn to love your husbands, too!

Act II   53

>   By stealing them!
>   Loves to hunt, she's a country girl, she's a witch!

Catherine of Aragon Nice young ladies
>   Feed you cakes and camomiles,
>   *This* young lady
>   Feeds you to the crocodiles!

All 5 Queens She will show contempt for wicked lies by telling them.
>   She'll assess the value of her friends by selling them.
>   You can judge the fragrance of her thoughts by smelling them!
>   She's a puss! She's a pet!
>   So we'd better get a vet!
>   Better yet,
>   Let's get
>   That bitch!

Elsewhere, Henry, Cromwell and Norfolk are still drinking together. Henry is enjoying the politically edgy situation which he is creating

Henry I have it in mind, Cromwell, to promote you to Chief Justice.
Cromwell I'm not worthy.
Henry Exactly! You are a notable scoundrel. Once you feel deserving and righteous, you'll be no use to the Law of England. (*He turns to Norfolk*) Uncle. You shall be responsible for peace in the North.
Norfolk (*contemptuously*) Peace!? (*He staggers drunkenly to his feet*) If only I could *fight* somebody! Why don't we knock the bloody Scots for six! I could scratch up a bit of an army.
Henry (*warningly*) I trust you not to arm yourself, Uncle. We are friends, remember?
Norfolk Friends! Of course, Your Majesty. (*He bows ironically*) I shall always remember that.
Cromwell (*to Norfolk*) And if you forget it, I can apply a liberal definition to the law of Treason.
Henry (*to Cromwell*) And if *you* forget it, the Tower of London is only a short trip from the Law Courts.
Norfolk There are many castles in the North with thick walls and men used to the weight of a spear. They may prove stronger than all your legal arguments.
Cromwell Your niece Anne had a close haircut, Norfolk. Take care it doesn't become a family fashion.
Henry (*pleased*) Gentlemen! We have every cause for a fast and wonderful friendship.

Norfolk Friendship is a beautiful thing!
Henry A thing no woman could possibly understand.
Cromwell It's working together that brings us so close.
Norfolk You get to know a man when you work with him.
Henry And when you plot against him, eh, Uncle?
Norfolk You get to know his strength and his weakness.
Cromwell The weak point ... at the back of his neck.
Norfolk I could use your power, Cromwell. But we can still enjoy a drink together!
Cromwell I could use your wealth, Norfolk. But thank God we can have an evening out!
Henry I can use you both, gentlemen! And will permit you to refill my glass. The toast is friendship!

The Queens are watching

Catherine of Aragon Touching! Such loyalty!
Anne Boleyn Soon they'll vomit. And tomorrow they'll brag about their hangovers.
Anne of Cleves I don't think they really like sex.
Anne Boleyn It doesn't give them that satisfying headache the next day.
Catherine of Aragon *That's* what he left you for, Jane.
Catherine Parr A night of nausea in the lavatories of Castle Howard...
Anne Boleyn A fumy hug from an old man who envies him...
Anne of Cleves And a lawyer who wants his job.

With his arms round Cromwell and Norfolk, Henry starts to sing

Song 18: The Very, Very Best of Friends

Henry
The formula for friendship
Is difficult to define.
As a matter of expediency,
We all use diff'rent ingredients.
Even so, I'll give you mine!

Friendship is a delicate state,
Mingling love and hope and hate!
A mixing of many unlikely blends!
It's born from what we intend to be!

Cromwell And killed by what we pretend to be.
Norfolk It's difficult in the end to be

Act II   55

Henry   The very, very best of friends.
All Three   We're the very, very best of friends, are we!
Henry   The very, very best of friends!
Cromwell   But whether we remain so depends
Henry   On whether it pays me dividends.
Norfolk   And if it does not, it quickly ends,
All   We're the very, very best of friends.

Norfolk   The fantasy of friendship's
                    Impossible to achieve!
                    Our desire for peaceful amity
                    Is predestined for calamity
                    It's so sad how men deceive!

Cromwell   Friendship is a perilous thing!
                    'Specially when your friend's the King!
                    It's hardly what sanity recommends.
                    To soothe and flatter his enemies
                    To know how lethal his venom is:
Henry   Whenever I kill my enemies
                    It leads to the arrest of friends!
Norfolk/Cromwell   We are very, very best of friends,
                    Are we -
                    Extremely wary best of friends!
Norfolk   Uncertain as the ladies he weds!
Cromwell   A trio of not-too-thoroughbreds!
Henry   As long as you two can keep your heads!
All Three   We are temporary best of friends!

Cromwell   The fallacy of friendship
                    Is obvious to the blind!
                    For our faith is somewhat shakeable
Norfolk   And relationships are breakable
Henry   (*threateningly*) And a friend is hard to find!

Cromwell   Friendship is a fatuous game!
                    Sycophancy's nicer name!
                    A sickness no reasoner comprehends.
                    The mating-call of democracies!
                    Hypocrisy of hypocrisies!
                    No wonder the aristocracy's
                    A viper-ridden nest of friends!

	We are worried and depressed by friends
	Are we -
	Our double-dealing stealing friends!
	Whatever misadventures befall,
	I doubt that such friends will heed the call!
Henry	And if they do not, God rot them all!
All Three	We're the very scary best of friends!
Henry	Friendship is so easy, you see,
	I help you and you help me!
Cromwell	A doctrine
	That every wise man commends.
Henry	If sinful persons corrupt our reign,
Norfolk	The regal duty is all too plain,
Henry	But given your loyalty, we'll remain
	The legendary best of friends!
Cromwell	Life's a never-ending test of friends!
	We find,
Norfolk	A never-ending test of friends!
Henry	(*suspiciously, to Cromwell and Norfolk*) To meet a man of honour is rare!
Cromwell	(*even more suspiciously*) And I can smell traitors ev'rywhere!
Norfolk	A quality which we three all share!
Cromwell	We are warily - scarily -
Henry	Very temporarily -
Norfolk	Yet somehow necessarily
All Three	The very, very best of friends!
	We're the very, very best of friends!

They all roar with hollow laughter. Norfolk and Cromwell both look a little nervously at Henry. Elsewhere, the Queens are in a group

Catherine Parr After Jane Seymour died in childbirth in his middle years, the King was—for a moment—quite alone. He needed a mother to look after him.
Jane Seymour I love him. I'm close to him... I *was* close to him. What's he doing?
Catherine Parr Looking for a mother ... to help care for the children.
Catherine Howard To help care for *him*.
Catherine Parr *And* his son!
Anne Boleyn Who is more of *girl* than my *daught*er!

A studious young boy, Edward, wanders by, reading a book

Act II

Jane Seymour You mean *our* son! That's *our* son! Edward. (*She looks at him anxiously*) But he's very pale!

Edward exits

The Queens watch Henry talking with Norfolk and Cromwell

Cromwell What His Majesty *needs*, my lord, is a marriage that is well thought out for once. (*To Henry*) You need a *family*.

One by one, they all look at Anne of Cleves

Norfolk You need a wife.
Cromwell The *perfect* wife.
Norfolk *And* mother.
Cromwell To fill the gap.
Norfolk Someone understanding.
Cromwell To heal the wounds.
Henry (*musing*) A perpetual mistress ... *and* a permanent friend? Do you really think such a creature exists? I must have asked myself that question a thousand times...

Song 19: The Perfect Woman (Reprise)

Henry	The perfect wife For the perfect man Is a difficult thing to see.
Wives	It's me!
Henry	A woman who'd build The perfect life For a difficult king like me!
Wives	That's me!
Henry	A lady of countless qualities, Too intricate to explain;
Wives	Explain!
Henry	The beauty of an Anne Boleyn,
Anne Boleyn	Aaah!
Henry	The wisdom of a Catherine,
The 3 Catherines	Aaah!
Henry	The gentleness...
Wives	Yes?
Henry	Of Jane,
Jane Seymour	(*simpering*) Oh, Henry!

The Others (*in contempt*) Huh!
Henry My Jane!
The Others (*mocking Jane*) Oh, Henry!
Henry She'll need to be a princess!
Cleves/Aragon *Me*!
Henry An angel!
Wives *Me*!
Henry A whore!
Boleyn/Aragon (*to Howard*) That's *you*, dear!
Henry And more!

All the Queens respond with excited girlie chat around the group—"What's he up to?", etc., but it's mainly unintelligible

Henry Where is she?
Catherine of Aragon I'm here!
Henry The perfect woman!
Anne Boleyn I'm here!
Henry And tell me,
Jane Seymour Yes, dear!
Henry Why can't I find her?
Wives I'm *here*!
Henry Am I blinder than other men?
Anne of Cleves Yes. You are!
Henry Do they know more than I?
Catherine Howard By far!
Henry Must all my life go by?
Wives How?
Henry Wondering who?
Wives Why?
Henry Wondering why?
Wives When?
Henry Trying to see
Wives What?
Henry In my mind's eye.
Wives Where?
Henry I see her so clearly,
Catherine Parr Really?
Henry Yes, really,
In my mind's eye.
She'll be blonde,
Blondes Ah!
Henry Or brunette,

Act II   59

Brunettes Ah!
Henry With blue eyes,
Blue Eyes Yes!
Henry And yet,
Wives Yes, yes!
Henry I really wouldn't mind
If they were brown!
Brown Eyes My eyes are brown!
Henry She'll be slender and tall,
Tall Ones *I'm* tall!
Henry Unless of course she's small!
Small Ones *I'm* small!
Henry And she'll wear her hair up,
Wives I *do*! (*They all push their hair up...*)
Henry Or down.
Wives (*...letting their hair down*) That, too!
Anne Boleyn Well, that narrows it down!
Henry I see her
Wives Yes?
Henry So clearly,
Wives Really?
Henry Well, nearly,

They all groan

Henry In my mind's eye.
Anne Boleyn A very limited space!
Henry No, I don't see her at all!

Another groan

And yet, I love her,
Catherine Parr He loves me!
Henry The perfect woman.
Catherine of Aragon He loves me!
Henry I'd love her
Catherine Howard You see!
Henry To be beside me,
Anne Boleyn I will!
Henry And to hide me
Catherine Howard I will!
Henry From loneliness,
Wives Oh, yes!

Henry   And save me from despair.
Anne of Cleves There, there!
Henry   But where is she?
Wives Here!
Henry   Where,
Wives Here!
Henry   Where?
Wives Here!
Henry   Where? The perfect woman
Wives That's me!
Henry   Isn't there!
Wives We're ev'rywhere!

Cromwell and Norfolk argue about the choice of a perfect wife for the King, with Cromwell singing and Norfolk speaking

Cromwell   A German?
Norfolk A what?!
Cromwell   The perfect woman!
Norfolk Are you mad?
Cromwell   A German,
Norfolk A Hun?!
Cromwell   For the alliance!
Norfolk Damn the alliance!
Cromwell   Your defiance
Norfolk How dare you!
Cromwell   Is typical.
Norfolk You pipsqueak!
Cromwell   But marriage for a king
Norfolk I'm his uncle!
Cromwell   Is not a simple thing!
Norfolk We've learned that!
Cromwell   We must take time!
Norfolk Right!
Cromwell   We must be wise!
Norfolk Quite!
              Using our heads!
Cromwell   Quite! Using our eyes!
Henry   I see her so clearly!
Wives Really?
Henry   Yes, really,
Wives *Really*!
Henry   In my mind's eye.

Act II   61

Norfolk She should be English!
Cromwell *Anything* but English!
           She could be Portuguese,
Norfolk Good God!
Cromwell   Or Spanish, with ease,
Norfolk We've done that!
Cromwell   Italian?
           No, they always talk too much!
Norfolk So do *you*!
Cromwell   Or if he'll take the chance,
Norfolk (*suspiciously*) *What* chance?
Henry   We could of course try France!
Norfolk (*aghast*) *Not* France!
Henry   She could even be Greek
Norfolk (*in despair*) *Greek*?
Henry   Or Dutch!
Norfolk Oh, my God!
Henry (*totally confused*) I see her so clearly,
Wives Yes?
Henry   Well, nearly,
Wives Yes?
Henry   In my mind's eye.
Wives Yes? Yes? Yes?
Henry   No, I don't see her at all!

A collective huge groan from the Wives. During the following, Henry, Cromwell and Norfolk speak simultaneously, with the Wives responding to Henry

Henry	**Cromwell/Norfolk**	**The 6 Wives**
And yet I love her,	Flemish! English!	
		He loves me!
The perfect woman.	Spanish! Rubbish!	
		He loves me!
I'd love her	German! Vermin!	
		You see?
To be beside me,	Irish! *Never*!	
		I will!
And to hide me	We will find her	
		I will!
From loneliness,	Somewhere—	
		Oh, yes!

And save me	Somehow	
From despair.	Somewhere—	
		There, there!
But where is she?	But where is she?	
		Here!
Where,	Where,	
		Here!
Where,	Where,	
		Here!
Where?	Where?	
		Here!
The perfect woman	The perfect woman!	
		That's me!
Isn't there!	She's there!	
	Somewhere!	
		I'm ev'ry where!

Norfolk claps Henry on the shoulder

Norfolk Why that coffin face, Henry?
Henry (*gloomily*) To think the young do so easily—namely, find a mate—what has so far cost me three wives, the severed head of a laughing lady, and the invention of an entire religion! And what have I got to show for it? *Nothing*! But a rebellious daughter and a sickly son!

Edward enters, reading another book

(*Part concerned, part angry*) Edward. So much study… It'll hurt your eyes. Go outside and ride a horse—or chase a girl—do something *useful*!

Edward is inert and not reacting at all

But Elizabeth is cantering on her hobby-horse, waving her sword, running, jumping, fighting imaginary battles, behaving exactly like a boy

(*Shouting at her*) Elizabeth! Get off that horse! You'll hurt yourself! Why can't you find a nice book to read?

Elizabeth canters off on her hobby-horse

Edward sits, pale, shuts his book, sighs, picks up a small doll and goes off whispering to it in a maternal fashion

Henry looks after Edward, extremely worried, as Norfolk and Cromwell

Act II   63

come on stage behind him, followed by two Servants bearing a large painting

Henry (*shaking his head*) Children!
Norfolk We've found her, Henry!
Henry (*absently*) Found who?
Cromwell The perfect woman!
Norfolk A perpetual mistress…
Cromwell *And* a permanent friend!
Norfolk (*to the servants*) Show him!

Henry is shown a highly flattering portrait of Anne of Cleves. Fanfare as he appraises it

Catherine Parr That's nice!
Anne Boleyn Rather large for the living-room.

Henry is immediately intrigued by the portrait

The Queens are now all revealed around the stage. In the movement that reveals them, Anne of Cleves is disclosed kissing a good-looking young Frenchman, Francis of Lorraine

Everyone looks at Francis and Anne of Cleves. They stop kissing. Francis moves away from Anne, alarmed

Cromwell A nice Dutch girl. A good Protestant. It's really time you made your religious position clear.
Norfolk (*laughing*) A Protestant girl! One in the eye for the Pope!

Henry is looking at Anne of Cleves, moving relentlessly towards her. Catherine Parr gets a long, white dress, a bridal gown that could also be a nightdress

Anne of Cleves (*starting to panic*) Why's he looking at me?
Catherine of Aragon He wants to marry you.
Anne of Cleves Well, I don't want to marry him!
Catherine Parr Whyever not?
Anne of Cleves I've got a friend. Francis of Lorraine's my friend. Aren't you? (*She looks round*)

But Francis, terrified, runs away

Catherine of Aragon Francis'll never *marry* you.
Anne of Cleves Why should I want to marry the King of England?
Jane Seymour Who *wouldn't*?
Catherine Parr Everyone does!
Anne Boleyn It's a desirable position for a girl.
Anne of Cleves *Francis* is my desirable position.

Henry is standing, staring at her

Anne of Cleves He's not going to ask me, is he?
Henry (*loudly*) You will do me the honour of becoming my wife.

Without waiting to hear the answer, he turns and walks US, *where he is dressed in a nightshirt by the gentlemen*

Anne of Cleves (*calling after him*) No!

But Henry doesn't hear. Anne of Cleves struggles madly with the other Queens, who grab her, hold her, and force her into the bridal nightdress. A big bed is trundled on US. *Henry is standing eagerly beside it ... as the other Queens wrestle with Anne of Cleves*

Catherine of Aragon You *can't* refuse!
Anne of Cleves (*shouting*) I just did! He won't enjoy it!
Anne Boleyn Oh, yes, he will!
Catherine of Aragon For a little while.
Anne of Cleves I'll make quite *sure* he doesn't enjoy it!
Jane Seymour How?
Anne of Cleves In my country we have a saying—"When a stubborn man meets a mad elephant in a narrow lane, one of them must get out of the way"!
Catherine Parr But how will you *do* it?
Anne of Cleves Like *this*! (*She turns and faces the audience. She pulls a horrible face, sticks out her stomach and makes herself look absolutely grotesque*)

Catherine Parr shoves a bridal veil over her face and Anne of Cleves limps off towards Henry. When she reaches him, he moves to her like a romantic lover. He takes off her veil. She looks at him, cross-eyed, and he starts back, appalled

Henry You're *not* beautiful!
Anne of Cleves Was I *meant* to be?
Henry Can I marry someone who's not beautiful? It's ridiculous!

Act II

Anne of Cleves Your letter said nothing about me being beautiful. It was all about yourself. How lonely you were... How the children need a mother. Nothing about me being beautiful at all! Why do you need your wife to be beautiful, Hal?
Henry So I can love her. And I detest being called Hal.
Anne of Cleves (*puzzled*) So—you can't love anyone who's not beautiful? That shows a strange lack of sexual imagination. *I'm* expected to love *you*, I suppose.
Henry Naturally.

Anne of Cleves walks round Henry, lifts his nightgown critically

Anne of Cleves You are not exactly a Holbein, Hal! Mit your stomach considerably distended—you're very fat, Hal—und your legs thickening und dimpling. Und your colour purple. Und your age vell on the vindy side of forty. (*She whistles*) Not so beautiful, exactly!
Henry You will love me for what I am.
Anne of Cleves What are you, exactly?
Henry I am a man!
Anne of Cleves A fact which makes you sexually attractive?

Henry looks at her, then storms to a corner of the stage where Cromwell is standing

Henry Who brought this woman here?
Anne of Cleves (*calling after him*) You did! And we're already engaged, remember?
Henry (*roaring*) Cromwell!
Cromwell (*nervously*) My Lord?
Henry Is the marriage contract signed?
Cromwell (*handing him a document*) It is. And may I be the first to congratulate you?
Henry (*looking at the document*) It's an insult! A towering insult to me, a King! (*He crumples the document and throws it on the floor*)
Cromwell What exactly is the insult, My Lord?
Henry Her ugliness! She's flaunting it like a banner! It's mutiny!

Upstage, Anne of Cleves gets into bed

Cromwell She has reasonable legs.
Henry She'd make a fine piano!

Anne of Cleves, sitting up in bed, starts to munch a cheese and onion sandwich

Cromwell Her teeth are white.
Henry So are tombstones! I could never be seen with her in public!
Cromwell (*obsequiously*) They say, My Lord, the homelier type of girl is more—er—grateful.
Henry I fear her gratitude may be the death of me.
Cromwell They say, my lord, all cats are grey in the dark.
Henry How can I board her? Do I have to?
Cromwell I'm afraid so. It's in the contract.
Norfolk (*mumbling*) Bloody silly things, contracts.
Cromwell But cheerily, my lord.
Henry What's cheerily?
Cromwell (*with a feeble grin*) No need to look at the mantelpiece when you're poking the fire. (*He gives Henry a cheerful clap on the shoulder*)

Cromwell exits

Henry ambles slowly towards the bed, like a man to the scaffold

The Lights cross-fade

Will Somers, strumming his lute, enters with a group of young Courtiers, laughing and gossiping together

1st Young Courtier So what say you, Will Somers, about His Majesty's latest dilemma?
Will Somers In four wise words, my lord, "Sooner 'im than me"!

They laugh as he sings with sly, gossip-mongering wickedness

Song 20: Henry Tudor

(*Singing*) By bringing this tempestuous princess to us,
The King hath done a deed that seems incestuous.
For this old duck, much more than any other,
Looks old enough to be the old man's mother!
When any monarch takes a queen -
Despite her royal regalia -
It still takes two to make success -
And one to make a failure!

There was a young Henry named Tudor,
When he saw a woman, he wooed her!

Act II   67

>   The second he viewed her,
>   He promptly pursued her,
>   His tactics could not have been cruder!
>   Fa-la-la-la!
>
>   Oh, oh, oh, Henry Tudor, Henry Tudor!
>   No king is shrewder,
>   Ruder or lewder
>   Than Henry Tudor.
>   Fa-la-la-la-la-la!
>
>   He prayed for a son to succeed him,
>   And that was the passion that keyed him!
>   A queen had to be dim
>   If she didn't heed him,
>   He swiftly made sure that she freed him!
>   Fa-la-la-la!
>
>   Oh, oh, oh, Henry Tudor, Henry Tudor!
>   No king is shrewder,
>   Ruder or lewder
>   Than Henry Tudor.
>   Fa-la-la-la-la-la!
>
>   He first married Catherine of Aragon,
>   A po-faced and pious old paragon!
>   If Queens were not mothers,
>   He soon lined up others.
>   Each year his obsession was farrer gone!

Will Somers now conducts the Company

Company   Fa-la-la-la!
                 Oh, oh, oh, Henry Tudor, Henry Tudor!
Will Somers No king is vainer,
                 And-or insaner
Company   Than Henry Tudor!
                 Fa-la-la-la-la-la!

Will Somers makes an upward key-change for each successive Queen

Will Somers Miss Anne Boleyn, next to be bedded,
                 Made sure before that to be wedded!
                 When wedding a king,
                 Please remember one thing:

It's as well to know where to "be-headed"!

The Courtiers roar with laughter

Company Fa-la-la-la!
Oh, oh, oh, Henry Tudor, Henry Tudor!
Will Somers There's never been a
Monarch who's meaner
Company Than Henry Tudor!
Fa-la-la-la-la-la!
Will Somers King Henry then married Jane Seymour,
A lady who thought he could be more.
Like each other wife,
Marriage cost her her life.
It's a shame fate could not make Jane see more!

More raucous laughter from the Courtiers

Company Fa-la-la-la!
Oh, oh, oh, Henry Tudor, Henry Tudor!
Will Somers No king's as awful,
Vain and unlawful
Company As Henry Tudor!
Fa-la-la-la-la-la!
Will Somers And now there's this lady from Flanders
Whom ev'ryone constantly slanders!
I fear with this marriage
She'll have a miscarriage -
Because Henry Tudor philanders!

Company (*gleefully*) Fa-la-la-la!
Oh, oh, oh, Henry Tudor, Henry Tudor!
Will Somers No king's as hated
Or over-rated
Company As Henry Tudor!
Fa-la-la-la-la-la!
Will Somers But that is the way
Tudors are!

Will Somers and his giggling group disappear into the shadows

The Lights change as a miserable Henry arrives at the vast matrimonial bed. Sitting up in bed and cheerfully eating a large sandwich, Anne of Cleves smiles at him

Act II

Anne of Cleves Henry, are you very sad I'm not beautiful?
Henry What're you eating?
Anne of Cleves A cheese and onion sandwich. My favourite—mit a little garlic! (*She burps*) My father told me "Never make love on an empty stomach"!
Henry (*in despair*) Cheese and onion! What *kind* of cheese?
Anne of Cleves Limberger... I suppose it *is* sad. That's why you asked no-one to the wedding. You are ashamed of me, Hal... because I have not got a pretty face. (*She sings her song, still eating the cheese and onion sandwich*)

During the song, Henry gets resignedly into bed with her

Song 21: Is Sad

(*Singing*) The world is such a pretty place,
Is sad.
I do not have a pretty face,
Is sad!
But I am pretty in my heart,
And that's the most important part!
But still, I'd like to have a lover, too!
Is sad, but funny, but true.

The world will never change for me,
Is sad.
A beauty I shall never be,
Is sad!
And so I'll stay the way I am,
An ugly duck from Amsterdam,
Unlikely to attract a likely lad!
Is true, is funny, is sad!

She looks at the miserable Henry

Cheer up, old fellow. All cats are grey in the dark! And you're not so good-looking, either!

(*Singing*) I do not ask for much,
And yet I must confess
I'd like to find a little love,
I cannot ask for less.

She lifts the bedclothes and looks under them at Henry

Not marvellous-looking! But a terrific great codpiece on you!

(*Singing*) Life has not always been my friend,
Is sad.
But I love ev'ry lovely day I've had.
I'm grateful for the things I've seen,
And all the things that might have been,
That might have made tomorrow's smile be glad!
Too bad they didn't,
Too bad they didn't
Is sad, they didn't,
Is sad!

Come on, Hal! You don't look at the mantelpiece when you're poking the fire!

With this, she leaps on Henry with a voracious sexual assault. Alarmed by this apparently hideous girl, he leaps out of bed and rings a huge handbell, summoning his Courtiers

The Courtiers run to him, putting on their dressing gowns

Henry (*roaring*) God forbid that a monarch of the realm should fail to do his duty, but enough is *enough*!

Song 22: Get Rid of Her! (Reprise)

(*Singing*) Get rid of her,
Get rid of her,
The filthy Flanders mare!
The features of a gargoyle
And the aura of a bear!
Her onions and her ugliness
Together, God forbid!
Today she leaves,
This sow of Cleves,
Of her I *must* be rid!

(*Roaring*) I'll be rid of her smell,
And her stinking breath as well!
Life with her would be hell
To endure!

Act II

He smiles at Catherine Howard

> Why do men suffer so?
> God, I'm damned if I know!
> It's a wonder that we grow
> So mellow and mature!

> (*Roaring again*) Get rid of her,
> Get rid of her,
> Disgusting Flemish witch!

He turns accusingly to Norfolk and Cromwell

> And one of you must answer
> How I *wed* this ugly bitch!

> A body like a pudding
> I'd be mad to jump amid!
> Her conversation proving
> She's a mental invalid!

He smiles again at Catherine Howard

> So any maid
> Who would be queen
> Had better make her bid!

Catherine, nudged forward by Norfolk, stands at Henry's side. Henry turns to Anne of Cleves for the last time

> Get rid of her!
> Get rid of her!
> Get rid,
> Get rid,
> Get rid!

Anne of Cleves pulls off the white dress and runs around the stage full circle as Henry finishes the song. As she circles the stage, back to looking beautiful but running like an Olympic contender, the other Queens cheer her on

Her homing port is Francis of Lorraine, who snatches her in his arms and rushes her off the stage

Henry sighs with relief as the Courtiers remove his nightgown and dress him in his hunting clothes. Henry starts to age visibly, his movements becoming perceptibly slower and more ponderous

(*Gradually calming down, muttering*) I wish we had a few sayings in *my* country! Dear God, is there no *limit* to the things a King must do for England? I mean, a man asks so *little*! So pitifully *little*! Only to be loved, respected, admired! To have his jokes laughed at, his success applauded, and his lapses constantly understood. Someone to love him through the gouts, the nasal blockages, agony of the back, loosening of the bowels and premature falling of the gut ... to find him each morning, half-razored, pale from the dearth of sleep and off rumbling to stool—mysteriously, agonizingly beautiful!

Gentlemen-at-Court enter, dressed as huntsmen. And Henry's hobby-horse comes on. One gentleman is carrying Henry's bow, another his sword

All he requires—a man's simple everyday basic need—is a creature *so* ravishing, men look at her with envy as though he's acquired the rarest picture—so *pure* that no-one else may touch her—and so *sinful* that she'll tie herself into a whore's knot for his every whim and fancy! Delicate as the first Spring blossom, and strong enough to lift him into bed when he's retching with old ale and Rhenish wine! A mother as biddable as a child, and a private, personal whore who is still a virgin from the Nursery, hot under his blankets, and cold as charity to the world around her!

A Gentleman brings Henry's two-handed sword and lifts it for him when he finds it too heavy

Someone who will be struck dumb at a man who can still lift a broadsword...

A gentleman hands Henry his bow and draws it for him when it's too hard for him to do it himself

Draw a bow ... and jump into the saddle like a young man.

A harness comes down from the flies. Henry is fastened into it and is swung onto the horse like an old sack. When he's mounted, Henry stares at the audience and shouts

Have none of you a *daughter*?

Catherine Howard has been hidden by the other Queens. Now she emerges wearing a diamond tiara and covered in jewels, looking like the young queen

Act II

she has just become. Major regal fanfare as Norfolk guides her to Henry's side. She looks up at him with eager, childlike admiration

Catherine Howard You ride like an angel, my lord.
Anne Boleyn Like a god! Isn't that the word you're searching for?

Henry looks down at Catherine Howard, visibly delighted

Henry I can still sit a horse, no matter how she kicks.
Catherine Howard You ride beautifully, Henry. You look so *young* today! So handsome! Come back early, won't you, my darling?
Henry Yes. We'll be alone this evening?
Catherine Howard Alone? Of course we will. Only some of my friends might stay for dinner. Thomas and some of the others. You want me to see my friends, don't you? My friends mean so much to me.
Henry (*looking at her; smiling indulgently*) Yes, of course.

The horse moves off with Henry on it

Catherine is waving after him

Catherine Howard Be careful, darling. Don't tire yourself out hunting. Save some of your strength for me!

There's a mirror and piles of new clothes for Catherine and jewels in a corner

Her teenage friends, including Thomas Culpepper, run in and stand round Catherine, laughing and admiring the new clothes Henry has bought her, and drinking Henry's wine

Catherine Howard holds up a dress and admires herself in the mirror

Catherine Howard *He* gave me that...
1st Girl Henry gave it to her.
Catherine Howard (*putting on another tiara*) And *this* to go with it.
Thomas Culpepper Must have cost a fortune!
Catherine Howard He's frightfully kind, really!
2nd Girl What do you have to do for it, Catherine?
Catherine Howard Admire his riding. Feel terribly sorry for him when he has a pain in his leg.
1st Girl (*insisting*) What *else*?
Catherine Howard *Nothing* else. The moment he gets into bed, he's fast

asleep and snoring! I tell you, it's very easy! (*She picks up a silk handkerchief*) Shall we play it?
Thomas Culpepper What?
Catherine Howard The Game!
1st Girl What about your Henry?
Catherine Howard He won't know.
2nd Girl Won't he catch us?
Catherine Howard Of course he won't. I told you. He's asleep.
1st Girl Why does he think we come here?
Catherine Howard To discuss my clothes. Oh, and play the lute a little!
1st Boy The lute! (*He does a few stately steps*) And dance an old-fashioned galliard.
Thomas Culpepper Does he know anything?
Catherine Howard Not half as much as old Nanny Ironmonger at Castle Howard! Poor Henry! *He's so innocent*! Now, who's going to be He?
1st Girl Do Eeny-Meeny-Miny-Mo!

Holding the handkerchief, Catherine dances round the group, pirouetting round and round and pointing

Catherine Howard Eeny Meeny Miny Mo…
1st Girl Catch a virgin by the toe…
Thomas Culpepper Rock her gently to and fro…
1st Girl Ow, it hurts, I love it so!
Catherine Howard O.U.T. Spells out, so out you must *go*!

She finds herself pointing her finger straight at Henry who has rejoined them: he's dressed in a gorgeously embroidered velvet dressing gown

Henry I was trying to sleep.
Catherine Howard Ssh, everyone.
Henry It doesn't matter. What were you doing?
Catherine Howard Only playing the game. (*She goes to him, kisses him*) Won't you play with us, Henry? Won't you?
1st Girl Henry can be He.
Henry (*puzzled*) He?
1st Boy It.
2nd Girl He, She, or It.

Catherine Howard sits down and blindfolds him with the silk handkerchief. Music starts under

Act II   75

Henry What do I have to do?
1st Girl Guess who it is!
Catherine Howard Guess who's kissing you!

Song 23: Ten Wishes

Young People We give you ten wishes
                 To try to meet your match.
                 If wishes were fishes,
                 How many could you catch?

During the game with the blindfolded Henry, Catherine flirts recklessly and outrageously with Thomas Culpepper, while Henry, thinking she is addressing him, blunders around, coaxed by Catherine's voice. He has to try and find Catherine by the sound of her voice. She keeps moving around. There are several near-misses as the nursery rhyme proceeds

                 Wish number one:
Catherine Howard I wish I could fly round the sun!
Young People Wish number two:
Catherine Howard I wish I were queen of Peru!
Young People Wish number three:
Catherine Howard I wish I lived under the sea!
Young People Wish number four:
Catherine Howard I wish I could see through a door!
Young People Wish number five:
Catherine Howard I wish we could all stay alive!
Young People Wish number six:
Catherine Howard I wish I could do magic tricks!
Young People Wish number seven:
Catherine Howard I wish God would show me round heaven!
Young People Wish number eight:
Catherine Howard I wish I were queen of my fate!
Young People Wish number nine:
Catherine Howard I wish that all water were wine!
Young People Wish number ten:
Catherine Howard I wish I could have my ten wishes again!

She lets Henry catch her

Henry (*chuckling*) I like this game! More! Sweet Kate! More!
Catherine Howard Then keep the mask on, Henry. And see if you can catch me again!

Catherine spins him round as the song starts up again. She kisses Culpepper fiercely on the mouth as the game resumes and Henry stumbles around groping in the empty air to find her

Young People Wish number one:
Catherine Howard I want to do things we've not done!
Young People Wish number two:
Catherine Howard I want to be wicked with you!

She kisses and caresses Culpepper provocatively only two or three feet away

Young People Wish number three:
Catherine Howard I want you to do things to me!
Young People Wish number four:
Catherine Howard I want to make love on the floor!

Culpepper, though nervous, is going crazy. The Young People are loving it. So is Catherine. And so, above all, is the unknowing Henry, as the music and the game becomes progressively wilder and more dangerous

Young People Wish number five:
Catherine Howard I want you to eat me alive!
Young People Wish number six:
Catherine Howard I want you to teach me new tricks!
Young People Wish number seven:
Catherine Howard I want you to ride me to heaven!
Young People Wish number eight:
Catherine Howard I want to be served on a plate!
Young People Wish number nine:
Catherine Howard I long for your tongue to touch mine!
Young People Wish number ten:
Catherine Howard I wish I could have my ten wishes again!
Young People We gave you ten wishes
　　　　　To try to meet your match.
　　　　　If fishes were wishes,
　　　　　How many did you catch?
Catherine Howard (*calmly, seductively, to Culpepper*) Did you enjoy that, my lord?

Culpepper silently nods

Henry I did, Catherine! I really *did*!
Catherine And so did I. From now on we must do it *much* more often!
2nd Girl Who was it?

Act II

1st Young Man Of *course* it was Catherine!
Henry (*standing up awkwardly*) What do I do *now*?
Culpepper Catch her!

Culpepper runs off into the shadows with a giggling Catherine Howard. We can see them kiss and disappear

1st Girl You have to catch her!

They all run off laughing into the shadows

Blindfolded, Henry is left alone—lurching around and grabbing at nothing. He gives a great howl of pain and loneliness

Cromwell comes in quietly and helps him untie the blindfold

Lighting change

Cromwell She has slept each night with Thomas Culpepper.
Henry I'll not believe it! You always hated her. She's a *child*! Admit it. You hated her, Thomas.
Cromwell A knowing child. Whose sin came with a nursery rhyme.
Henry A knowing child. That was why I loved her.
Cromwell Love. They only use "Lust". It's their only word.
Henry How can I condemn her? For being the thing I wanted?
Cromwell If you're sure she's done wrong, you *must* condemn her! Legally.
Henry *Sure*? How can I be sure?

The sound of the Young People laughing off stage

Cromwell She's laughing at you!

The Young People come running in. They are holding huge fantastic masks and cloaks. The main masks represent the Signs of the Zodiac

The sound of music for the masque as all the Courtiers, with the Queens as part of the court, come in and try on the masks and costumes

The Young People are laughing. Henry and Cromwell are watching them

Cromwell They're *all* laughing at you!
Henry It's their *age*! They laugh at *everything*!
Cromwell Because *you* sleep while *she* wriggles in bed with Culpepper!

Henry I can't be *sure*!
Cromwell While she sits beside you at dinner, he has his hand up her skirt.
Henry True, I have sometimes seen her squirm at the table … I thought in delight at the roast meats!
Cromwell In delight at his fingers!
Henry If I could be sure…
Cromwell The masque will make you sure. Put on a mask, My Lord. How else can you hope to learn the truth?
Henry I'm in no mood for masking, Thomas.

Henry and Cromwell turn and are hidden in the crowd. The whole stage is full of people dressing for the masque. When they are dressed, most of the characters are unrecognizable with full masks, covering their heads completely, and long cloaks. All except for Catherine Howard as the Moon. She carries a small mask so we can recognize her

Catherine Howard (*whispering to Capricorn*) I know it's you, Thomas. They all told me you were going to play the goat.

Fanfare of trumpets

  A masked Sun King with attendant Nymphs descends in a golden chariot from the flies. When the chariot touches the ground, the Sun King gets out

Everyone applauds

(*To Capricorn*) Poor Henry! He's so ridiculous! He can never resist an entrance.

The Sun King leads a masked Moon Queen out to dance. Catherine Howard is dancing with Capricorn, whispering in his goat's ear

Tonight, Thomas, I'll come to you tonight. What's the matter? You're not afraid, are you? Not scared? You aren't usually. It'll be a good game. *All* the best games are a bit scary. Anyway, he'll sleep tonight. He'll sleep so soundly. He always does. And this is late for the old man to be up. Nine o'clock. Long past his bed-time. You know, he always told me such stories. All about the wives and mistresses he's slept with. (*She laughs*) I'm sure that's exactly what he did. Sleep. Look at him! Doesn't he look *ridiculous*? He imagines he's the Sun! Poor old Sun! He has no idea what the world gets up to after he's gone to bed at night!
Henry (*grimly*) Alas for you, he *does*, sweet Kate.

Henry takes off the Capricorn mask and reveals himself. Two soldiers seize

Act II

the Sun King and pull off his mask. He's Thomas Culpepper. The Moon Queen takes off her mask. Under it is another mask. A grinning mask. Henry moves to Culpepper and looks at him with contempt

Your five minutes of being king are over!

Thomas Culpepper looks back at Henry steadily

Thomas Culpepper As are *your* five minutes of being a young man!

Henry turns and on his way out gestures at Catherine without looking at her

Henry Get rid of her!
Catherine Howard No! Henry!

Henry ignores her and strides out

Catherine holds out her arms to him in a futile plea. The stage is prepared for her execution—a grim reprise of her cousin Anne Boleyn's fate at the end of Act I. Contemplating her fate, she sings like a child of her lost broken dreams

Song 24: The Wishing Tree

(***Singing***) If life could be a wishing tree,
My hopes would blossom ev'ry year.
La-la-la-la-la-la-la-la,
La-la-la-la-la-la.

If hope could be a bumble-bee,
Its friendly buzz is all I'd hear.
And if life were a wishing tree,
There'd be nothing to fear.

If fear could be a fantasy,
My dreams of death would disappear.
And if life were a wishing tree,
There'd be nothing to fear.

And if hope were a bumble-bee,
There'd be nothing to fear.
There'd be nothing to fear.

A guard enters and stands threateningly over her

Go away, please. I'm not ready for you yet.

The Lights cross-fade to Will Somers and Norfolk leaving the place of execution

Will Somers You must be running a bit short of nieces, Uncle Norfolk.
Norfolk (*matter-of-factly*) Not really, no. The Norfolks breed like rabbits. Plenty more where those came from.

Will strums his lute and sings to the audience

Song 25: Henry Tudor (Reprise)

Will Somers Kate Howard, number five, came from Norfolk,
Them Norfolk girls surely don't bore folk!
Like Annie, her cousin,
'Twas men by the dozen
You can't say the Norfolks abhor folk!
Fa-la-la-la!

Catherine Parr comes on and stares at Will Somers disapprovingly

(*Confidentially*) Bizarre mistress Parr, she's a myst'ry!
With Henry, she's brother and sistery!
The first five were acid,
P'raps this one's more placid,
But all six together are hist'ry!
Company Fa-la-la-la!
Oh, oh, oh! Henry Tudor, Henry Tudor!
Will Somers No king's more ruthless,
Toothless and truthless
Company Than Henry Tudor!
Fa-la-la-la-la-la!
But that is the way Tudors are!

The music and the Courtiers fade away in the distance as a suddenly elderly Henry enters arm-in-arm with Catherine Parr, who escorts and pampers him like a nurse

The other Queens watch them. They are joined by Catherine Howard, now also in a black dress, with a thin red ribbon at her neck

Act II

Henry (*very tired*) Do you want to marry me, Catherine Parr? (*Aside*) Another Catherine!? God's teeth, I must be mad!
Catherine Parr I think it's best, don't you? Marriage is the right true end of love.
Henry It's the right true end of a lot of other things, too! (*His mind wanders into a confused, disconnected reminiscence*)

His various Queens gather around him

Do you remember Nonesuch, Catherine? We were like two lovebirds, locked in a golden cage.
Catherine of Aragon I always wanted to make you happy, Henry.
Henry Well, here's your opportunity. Consent to the divorce.
Catherine of Aragon If I let you go—what will be left to me?
Henry You've got your religion, and all the new books that are coming up. Perhaps you could take up gardening.
Catherine of Aragon Why don't you tell *her* to take up gardening! I hear she has six green fingers!
Henry Names! Tell me their names.
Anne Boleyn Norris and Weston in my bed, and Brereton under the stairs. Thomas.
Henry Thomas?
Anne Boleyn Thomas Wyatt. Times without number.
Henry You whore! You lying, treacherous whore! Would you spit on your marriage vows? Is there no faith left? No true love anywhere?
Anne Boleyn So I have had my little Smeaton, and you your little Seymour.
Henry It's not the *same*! Ah! Jane Seymour... *She* was the one! In retrospect, the perfect wife. Boring, but good. With her I could have had as many mistresses as I could cope with. She was too good and too boring to even notice! But all she did was give me a boring son and then *die*, stupid woman!

The Lights cross-fade to a sad and lonely Jane Seymour. Henry smiles at her as the music starts under

Song 26: The End of Love

Jane Seymour The start of love is sweet,
   A rare and precious thing;
   When ev'ry day is spring
   And you're the friend of love.
Anne Boleyn That part of love is good,
   It's like a lovely game!

      It can't and never should
      Stay the same.
Catherine of Aragon Then all at once it's changed,
      Your life is rearranged,
      There's much we can't pretend
      To comprehend
      Of love.
Catherine Howard But still the game goes on,
      Though what you seek is gone,
      And that is that,
      The end of love.
Catherine Parr You can't reverse the trend of love,
      Especially the end of love.
The Queens But still the game goes on,
      Though what you seek is gone,
      And that is that,
      The end of love.
      You can't reverse the trend of love,
      Especially the end of love.

The Lights cross-fade back to Henry

Catherine Howard Henry! Henry!
Henry God have Mercy! Where do you think you're going?
Catherine Howard To bed. It's past my bedtime.
Henry What games are you playing?
Catherine Howard Nursery rhyme games ... games for children. Where was Moses when the light went out?
Henry I don't know.
Catherine Howard In the dark.
Jane Seymour Where have you been?
Henry I told you. Staying with my Uncle Norfolk.
Jane Seymour Did you enjoy yourself?
Henry Not very much. I should have been with you.
Jane Seymour It's nothing ... only a little pain ... only a little.
Henry I should never have left you, Jane.
Jane Seymour It was perfect, Henry. Remember? And I gave you your son!
Henry That's what I want. A son.
Jane Seymour Why did you go away, Henry? Weren't we happy together? *Weren't* we?
Henry A son. Does it kick like a boy, then? Does it?
Jane Seymour Didn't you *want* to be happy?
Henry Farris will make him a suit of armour.

Act II   83

Jane Seymour Couldn't you believe in anything so simple?
Henry I'll get him some ponies sent out of Wales.
Jane Seymour Henry, *look* at me!
Henry We'll hunt the red deer together...
Jane Seymour It's me ... *Jane*! Don't you *want* a wife? Didn't you *ever*?
Henry He will be *me*! Always! Running out ... into the future!
Jane Seymour Hold my hand, Henry. Hold it *now*!

Song 27: A Man is About to be Born

Henry I've lived my life to the full,
To the brim,
And people one day
May laugh and say
There never was ever
A fool like him!

But at least they will remember,
As much as people can,
That once there lived a king,
A vain and foolish king,
Who learned through pain and suffering
To be a man.

A man is about to be born,
And soon overhead will be dawning
The start of a beautiful morning,
To adorn the summer sky.

A life is about to begin,
And into his little tomorrow,
A man pours his love and his sorrow,
But he needs a reason why.

Why does he live? Why does he die?
Why does he laugh and cry?
What does he know, where can he go?
What can he do but try?

The day is beginning to dawn,
The future is waiting before me,
And fate will acclaim or ignore me.
Will my day be gray or bright?
Will I win or lose the fight?

> Out of the darkness—into the light:
> A man is about to be born!

The sound of a distant crowd cheering and bells ringing. Fireworks

Henry My son! At *last*! My *son*!
Catherine of Aragon The rejoicing was particularly great.
Anne Boleyn So much so that the mother was neglected.
Catherine Parr She died twelve days after the baby was born.
Henry My *son*! The celebrations! Wine in the fountains...
Catherine of Aragon A hundred oxen roasted in the fields of Piccadilly.
Catherine Parr A thousand choir boys singing the *Te Deum*.
Anne Boleyn Free hog meat for the poor.
Catherine of Aragon All Church bells rung by order.
Catherine Parr Bonfires from Land's End to John O'Groats.
Catherine Howard Free pardon for all criminals awaiting trial.
Anne of Cleves A clean pair of sheets for all brides certified virginal...
Anne Boleyn ...And a bucket of coal for the elderly.
Catherine Parr Compulsory loyal toasts to be drunk in all Government departments...
Catherine Howard ...And compulsory throwing of hats in the air on all streets between Cheapside and Ludgate...
Catherine of Aragon To celebrate His Majesty's historic achievement!
Anne Boleyn He rolled over in a warm bed, felt the soft side of a buttock and sleepily discharged two million spermatozoa in a vague hope of immortality.
Anne of Cleves Don't you think that calls for a ripple of applause?

The Queens clap faintly, except for Jane, who cheers as London's church bells ring loudly in the background

Jane Seymour The birth of a son! The right true end of love!
Henry A son! Man's greatest achievement... Man!

The sound of redoubled cheering, etc. Edward, now in a black suit, closes the book he is reading

Song 28: Sextet/Young Together

Catherine of Aragon A brash and brutal prince was he,
    And I was his one real queen!
Anne Boleyn If he had been as brave as I,
    Oh, what he might have been!

Act II   85

Catherine of Aragon Might have been…
Catherine of Aragon/Anne Boleyn Might have been!
Jane Seymour A lost and lonely prince was he,
          A man nobody knew.
Anne of Cleves I know I could have loved him well
          If he had loved me, too!
Anne Boleyn Loved me, too!
Anne of Cleves/Jane Seymour Loved me, too!
Anne Boleyn/Jane Seymour Loved me, too! Loved me, too!
Catherine Howard A vain and vicious prince was he,
          Who tore my life apart.
Catherine Parr His days will end unhappily
          Because he has no heart.
All   Has no heart.
Anne Boleyn Has no heart.
All   Has no heart.
Catherine of Aragon Has no heart.

The music segues to Henry rambling wistfully in his dotage

Henry   We were young together,
          We were springtime,
          We began together,
          And we ran together,
          Through the golden days
          Of youth.

          And in truth together,
          We were happy,
          For we dreamed together
          And it seemed together
          We would see the years go by.
          But the golden days have flown,
          And I wander on alone.
Henry/Wives We were young together,
          You and I.
Catherine Parr When a man and a woman grow old… When they hug their knees to the fire, for they are too spent for hunting, and suck the bone, for they are blunt-toothed and cannot chew the flesh…
Henry (*noticing Anne of Cleves*) Wasn't I married to *her* once?
Catherine Parr (*patiently*) Yes, dear, I expect so.

Henry Never tumbled her, though. *Why* didn't I ever tumble her? (*He remembers*) Oh, I know why! Because I thought she was ugly ... and she *was*! She was hideous! And she ate those awfully smelly sandwiches! That was it! Well, I mean, you can't really *blame* me, can you?
Catherine Parr (*comforting him*) No, dear. Not at all.
Henry Oh dear, oh dear! So many mistakes ... so many ridiculous mistakes!
Catherine Parr Settle down now, dear. You need a good rest.
Henry What's good about a rest? I won't make the same mistake this time. I've learnt now ... learnt my lesson. Jane ... I should have looked after Jane. She was what I was after ... the love of a true wife. Of course, there'll still be a few adventures behind the hedges ... on the wrong side of the curtain. Anne, the sorceress, and that little Howard! She'd have been worth a tumble, if I'd gone into it with my eyes open. Not taken it so *seriously*... And Catherine ... Catherine of Arrogant! We could have been *two kings* together, Catherine and I! And Anne, dear Dutch Anne. So beautiful, in a funny sort of way. But I'll make it up to her. I'll make it up to *all* of them! I'll do it *right* this time ... everything I missed. I'm ready now ... just ready to start. (*He falls asleep on Catherine Parr's shoulder*)

She gently serenades him

Song 29: Finale
The Grape and the Vine (reprise)

Catherine Parr   As the grape will cling to the vine,
                As the vine will cling
                To the walls of the house,
                As the house will cling to the earth,
                And the earth to the sea,
                I will cling to thee, my love,
                I will cling to thee.

                I vow to be thine,
                And thou be mine.
                Like the grape and the vine, my love,
                Like the grape and the vine.

The Lights slowly cross-fade as Will Somers enters with his lute and sings softly as the full Company gathers around him

Henry Tudor (reprise)

Will Somers And that is the true Tudor story,

Act II

        Amusing, bemusing and gory!
        King Hal was a monarch
        Whose problems were chronic,
        You can't overload him with glory!

        But that was
Company Henry Tudor! Henry Tudor!
        There was no ruler
        Weaker or crueller
        Than Henry Tudor!
        Fa-la-la-la-la-la!
Will Somers But that is the way Tudors are!

The voices of the singers gradually subside, and all the people disperse, leaving only the sleeping Henry

The Lights cross-fade to reveal the back wall of the stage dominated now by the famous William Segar ermine portrait of Queen Elizabeth the First

My Son! (reprise)

Henry (*voice over, gently*) A lover of the arts,
        A spirit bold and free,
        A hold on people's hearts
        That is incredible to see
        Has she! Has she!

        Beloved of the gods,
        Determined and defiant,
        Possessed of ev'ry gift and grace.
        A king, a giant!

Orchestra only, next 2 bars

        And ev'ryone who meets her
        Will readily agree:
        She's the one
        Who's exactly like me!
        She's born to be
        My son.

Henry's voice fades away into the distance. He continues sleeping

The music builds triumphantly as Elizabeth herself makes a regal entrance in front of the portrait. She is dressed identically as in the portrait. She bears a startling resemblance to, and sings with the unmistakable voice and clarity of purpose of her late mother, Anne Boleyn

I'm Not! (reprise)
Elizabeth Women are afraid to be
Half the things they're made to be,
Why are they ashamed to be
All the things I've aimed to be?
I'm not! I'm not!

My ideas on life,
Papa would find obscene!
But Mother would be happy
That I'm called the Virgin Queen!

With steely contempt, she looks down at the sleeping Henry

Let other monarchs
Get their lives go by!
I'm not!
Not I!

A gloriana fanfare as she walks slowly, majestically US *towards her portrait and her destiny, and the Light focuses in smaller and tighter on the sleeping figure of Henry—*

—and the CURTAIN *falls*

FURNITURE AND PROPERTY LIST

Further dressing may be added at the director's discretion

Prologue

On stage: Holbein portrait of **Henry**

ACT I

On stage: Clothes-rack with scarlet dress
Bed containing pillows, covers and small bundle

Off stage: 6 regal costumes (**SM**)
Head-dress (**Catherine Parr**)
Mirror (**Catherine Parr**)
White bridal veil (**Wives**)
White jacket (**Wyatt, Wolsey, Norfolk**)
Huge crucifix (**Monks**)
Nightgown (**Anne Boleyn**)
Document (**Catherine of Aragon**)
Lute (**Smeaton**)
Glass of drink (**Norfolk**)
Lute (**Will Somers**)
Crown (**Gentlemen**)
Huge and heavy crown (**Wolsey**)
Pair of antlers (**Catherine Parr**)
Henry's hunting garb, spears, bows, red colouring for spear (**Courtiers**)

Personal: **Henry:** hat
Anne Boleyn: thin scarlet ribbon

ACT II

On stage: Block
Axe
Small doll
Huge handbell

Off stage: Lute (**Will Somers**)
Table with candlesticks and wine (**SM**)
Book (**Edward**)
Hobby-horse (**Elizabeth**)
Large painting of **Anne of Cleves** (**Servants**)
Long, white dress (**Catherine Parr**)
Nightshirt (**Gentlemen**)
Big bed with cheese and onion sandwich (**SM**)
Henry's hunting clothes, bow, sword (**Courtiers**)
Harness (**SM**)
Mirror, piles of new clothes, jewels, tiaras, silk handkerchief (**SM**)
Huge fantastic masks, cloaks (**Young People**)
Golden chariot with masked **Sun King** and **Nymphs** (**SM**)
Portrait of **Queen Elizabeth** (**SM**)

Personal: **Cromwell:** document
Catherine Howard: thin red ribbon

LIGHTING PLOT

Property fittings required: nil
Various interiors/exteriors

PROLOGUE

To open:	Lighting on **Henry** and painting	
Cue 1	**Henry** sings *Bring lights up on* **Queens**	(Page 1)

ACT I

To open:	Overall general lighting	
Cue 2	**Anne Boleyn**: "With you, he behaved like one!" *Fade lights*	(Page 4)
Cue 3	Fanfare grows louder, more majestic *Golden shaft of light on* **Henry**	(Page 4)
Cue 4	**Catherine Parr**: "It was quite a ceremony." *Change lighting*	(Page 10)
Cue 5	**Henry**: "…clawing at each other's throats!" *Change lighting to denote passage of time*	(Page 10)
Cue 6	**Anne Boleyn** hurries away *Fade lights to darkness*	(Page 11)
Cue 7	**Catherine of Aragon** is heard in angry Spanish. *Bring lights back up*	(Page 11)
Cue 8	**Queens** group around **Catherine of Aragon** *Darken lights*	(Page 15)

Cue 9	**Chorus** sing *Change lighting*	(Page 23)
Cue 10	Music and dancing end suddenly *Change lighting*	(Page 25)
Cue 11	**Henry** walks into shadows *Light on* **Jane Seymour** *and* **Anne Boleyn**	(Page 26)
Cue 12	**Anne Boleyn** reveals scarlet ribbon *Fade to darkness, and back up during action*	(Page 26)
Cue 13	**Smeaton** sees **Norfolk** *Rapidly fade lights to darkness*	(Page 37)
Cue 14	**Smeaton**: "And have committed … fornication!" *Bring up lights*	(Page 37)

ACT II

To open:	Overall general lighting	
Cue 15	**Henry** drinks greedily *Golden light on* **Jane**, *then general lighting*	(Page 49)
Cue 16	**Norfolk**: "…the bedroom and the battlefield!" *Focus lights on* **Queens**	(Page 51)
Cue 17	**Henry** ambles slowly to bed *Cross-fade to* **Will Somers**	(Page 66)
Cue 18	**Will Somers** and his group exit *Cross-fade to* **Henry** *at bed*	(Page 68)
Cue 19	**Cromwell** helps **Henry** with blindfold *Change lighting*	(Page 77)
Cue 20	**Catherine Howard**: "I'm not ready for you yet." *Cross-fade to* **Will Somers** *and* **Norfolk**	(Page 79)
Cue 21	**Henry**: "…and then die, stupid woman!" *Cross-fade to* **Jane Seymour**	(Page 81)

Lighting Plot

| Cue 22 | **Queens**: "Especially the end of love." | (Page 82) |
| | *Cross-fade back to* **Henry** | |

| Cue 23 | **Henry**: "A man is about to be born!" | (Page 83) |
| | *Fireworks effect* | |

| Cue 24 | **Catherine Parr**: "Like the grape and the vine." | (Page 86) |
| | *Slowly cross-fade to* **Will Somers** | |

| Cue 25 | **People** disperse, leaving sleeping **Henry** | (Page 87) |
| | *Cross-fade to portrait of* **Queen Elizabeth** | |

| Cue 26 | **Queen Elizabeth** walks to painting | (Page 88) |
| | *Focus on sleeping* **Henry** | |

EFFECTS PLOT

ACT I

Cue 1	**Wyatt**: "Thomas Wyatt, the friendly friend." *Sound of bell ringing*	(Page 7)

ACT II

Cue 2	**Henry**: "A man is about to be born!" *Sound of distant crowd cheering and bells ringing, fireworks effect*	(Page 84)
Cue 3	**Anne of Cleves**: "…calls for a ripple of applause?" *Sound of London's church bells ringing loudly in background*	(Page 84)
Cue 4	**Henry**: "Man's greatest achievement… Man!" *Sound of redoubled cheering, etc.*	(Page 84)

www.ingramcontent.com/pod-product-compliance
Lightning Source LLC
LaVergne TN
LVHW051750080426
835511LV00018B/3289